About Self-publishing

An essential guide

for new authors

By

Allie Cresswell

© *Allie Cresswell, 2023. Except as provided by the Copyright Act [1956, 1988, 2003] no part of this publication may be reproduced, stored in a retrieval system or transmitted in any form or by any means without the prior written permission of the publisher.*

Allie Cresswell asserts her moral rights to be identified as the author of this work.

Contents

Introduction and Disclaimer 5
1. Writers are Readers 7
2. Some Hard Facts 9
3. Indie Writers Are Networkers 11
4. Write Your Book 13
5. 'The End' is only The Beginning 17
6. Traditional or Self-Publish? 20
7. The Road to Self-Publishing 25
8. The Book 26
9. Formatting for Upload to KDP (Kindle Direct Publishing) 36
10. Going Wide 56
11. Launch 63
12. Putting it All Together 80
13. Jargon Busting Glossary of Terms. 89
About the Author 94
Also by Allie Cresswell 95

Introduction and Disclaimer

I don't pretend to be an expert in anything. My technical know-how is only what I have picked up by trial and error. I'm not a publicist or a marketing guru. I'm sure there are courses you can do that will show you how to format and launch your book better than I can, and there are paid-for services which will do the whole thing for you.

Having said all that, I have successfully self-published fourteen novels now, and over the years I have honed a process that works for me. That's what I'm going to share in this short book. It works for *me*, but I make no guarantees that it will work for you. I'm learning all the time and, of course, the marketplace, publishing platforms and social media are ever-evolving. What is true for me today might not be true for anyone tomorrow. However, we all have to start somewhere, so why not learn from my experience as you map your own journey to publication?

I've loved writing stories for as long as I can remember but I began my first novel, *Game Show*, in 1992. It took me ten years to write between raising the kids and working both inside and outside the home. I was successful in getting an agent for it but she couldn't place it and when books two and three went in different directions we agreed to part ways. I failed to get representation for my subsequent works and in the end I self-published on zero budget, with off-the-shelf covers, no editorial support, no 'launch' and no promotional budget. Sales, needless to say, were woeful although the reviews I got were very good.

I began my sixth book, *Tall Chimneys*, with the gloomy premonition it would be my last, but a good friend encouraged me to enter it into the Kindle Scout competition. I did so, and spent a month urging everyone I knew even vaguely to vote for it. It wasn't successful, but on publication day I got 1600 downloads and that kicked some Amazon **algorithm**[1] into action. Sales were GREAT. They didn't last, but the funds generated allowed me to go back to previous books and improve them.

I joined an indie writers' group called One Stop Fiction, and that's where I began to pick up some of the tips that I have subsequently honed to create the book launch system I'm going to share with you here. Sadly, One Stop Fiction in its original form is obsolete now but I have remained friends with some of the brilliant indie writers I met there.

To date, my lifetime sales across a catalogue of 14 books and two anthologies are nearly 60,000, plus 18.5 million page reads via Amazon's Kindle Unlimited program. This is nothing in the wider scheme of things, but in the field of independent publishing, and over a period of a few years, I think it's okay.

---

[1] Terms in bold are explained in the glossary.

1. Writers are Readers

One of the problems with self-publishing is that, in some ways, it is *too* easy. Every day thousands of books enter the marketplace—books that are not well-written or properly edited, with amateurish covers and hackneyed storylines. I don't want to add to that swamp and this book is not about encouraging you to do that either.

My first challenge to you is to READ.

Read the classics, read good-quality books by highly respected authors. Look up the '100 books you must read before you die' list and tick off the ones you've read, then work your way through some of the others. Reading good books will make you a better writer.

I have been an avid reader for as long as I can remember. I had read my way through the children's library by the time I was ten years old and was allowed the great privilege of borrowing books from the adult section (under Mum's supervision) a year before I began secondary school. Mum was my biggest role model in turning to books for escape, for information and for entertainment. Her chair always had a book on its arm. She would bring a book to read in the car while she waited for us to come out of school, to dentist and doctor appointments—anywhere there might be a five-minute opportunity to read.

As I grew up she bought me books she had enjoyed as a younger woman. Hence, I still enjoy returning to the works of Norah Lofts, Elizabeth Gouge, Daphne du Maurier, AJ Cronin and RL Delderfield. These writers are not widely enjoyed nowadays but their books are wonderful, and I love trawling through second-hand bookshops to pick up copies that others have let go.

Once at secondary school and then later at university I began to read the nineteenth century classics that are still my go-to favourites: Austen, Dickens, Trollope, Wharton and the

Brontës. Nowadays I also read contemporary writers who produce quality writing—writers who are not afraid to use three words rather than one when those three words add layers of flavour and substance. My favourite modern writers are Olivia Hawker, Emma Donoghue and Elisabeth Strout. If I could write a quarter as well as any of those women, I'd die happy.

I love a good story, not to mention relatable characters, but on the whole I like books that are 'gourmet' as opposed to 'fast-food.'

Essentially, I read the books that I would like to write, and I write the books I would like to read.

By reading the books of writers they admire, would-be writers can see where the benchmark is set. Reading analytically—thoughtfully—brings understanding of what those writers are doing that makes their books so good. If they happen to be critically acclaimed *and* popular bestsellers, all the better; it demonstrates what readers are looking for and what sells well. The very best way to get a handle on both the excellent and the less successful aspects of a book is to write a review. It really concentrates the mind. Only a published writer can properly appreciate how important readers' reviews are.

Personally, I don't write to market—that is, I don't jump on a best-selling bandwagon. The market is flooded with wannabe JK Rowlings, and no one will ever out-Tolkien Tolkien. Plus, readers are wise to books that are pale imitations of classic best-sellers and runaway success new releases. They know a worn-out trope when they see one. If a book is just a rehashed facsimile of a big-hitter it will have no integrity. Like that squirty cream you can buy, it might look good for a few minutes but after that you have a pool of greasy-looking liquid on the plate. It's artificial, and readers will instantly know it.

Be authentic.

I write my own books from my own heart, but am inspired by the writers I love. I don't try to replicate their books but do aspire to reach their level of skill.

2. Some Hard Facts

I read recently that most **indie** writers expect to sell fewer than 250 books across their entire catalogue—a discouraging statistic when you think about the 'million-copy best-selling' banners on the books that top the New York Times Best-Seller list. But I think of it this way. If my children had 250 real friends I'd be thrilled. I'd be justified in calling them popular and successful. So 250 people who are prepared to pay for my books is pretty good.

For me, the satisfaction of writing is its own reward. I derive an income from my writing but it couldn't sustain me. Luckily, I don't do it for the money. I write because I can't *not* write. So here is my next challenge to you.

Do you write because you must? If your main aim is to make money, win plaudits or gain celebrity, I suggest you think again.

Of course, your book may be amazing. It might get snapped up by an agent and optioned by Netflix. You might find yourself on the circuit of book fairs and literary events giving readings and doing book signings. It happens for some writers, so why not you? I really hope you make it, but I caution you that you might not. And then I guess you'll have to ask yourself—as I have—has it been worth it? Have the thousands of hours I poured into these novels of mine been well-spent? If I had my time over, would I do it again?

My answer to that question is a resounding YES. My first marriage wasn't very happy but I got two amazing children from it. I'd do the full twenty-five years all over again for their sake. It's the same with my books.

Over one million books are published every year in the US alone. In 2018 it was estimated that there were over 1.6 million of us indie authors all fighting for breathing space in the market. The sad fact is that while some writers are fortunate enough to be successful—often more a matter of luck than anything else—those of us who are not celebrities or who miss out on that rare big break must content ourselves with labouring alone in obscurity. The good news is that there are lots of us. We are a tribe.

3. Indie Writers Are Networkers

In addition to reading books by mainstream or established writers, I like to delve into books in my favourite genres by indie authors. At the very least I'll know what I'm up against in the marketplace but in the best-case scenario I might find a friend. We indie writers can make each other's lonely writing lives quite enjoyable if we encourage and assist one another—hence this book.

There are numerous writing groups on social media where indie writers—also agents, editors, cover designers and publicists—are keen to make the indie world a better place to be. Join one. Or two.

Further on in this book we'll talk about beta readers, launch teams and blog tours, but in reality all of that starts right here.

It's worth gathering your tribe around you from the get-go.

One way to start this is to drop an email to the writer of an indie novel you've enjoyed. They invariably provide a means of getting in contact. Check the author page or the copyright information; they may have a website. Tell them you enjoyed their book and why. Send them a link to the glowing review you posted. Make friends. Follow some book bloggers in your genre on Facebook, Twitter or Instagram and engage meaningfully with their posts. When you need them, hopefully they'll be there for you.

Social media is a gamechanger in allowing us to reach out into the world and make connections. Begin to establish 'writer' you as distinct from 'real' you. Think about this and then write a **bio**. It can only be rudimentary at this point, but begin to establish *why* you want to write and *what kind* of writer you will be. Set up a dedicated author website, business Facebook page, Twitter and Instagram accounts. Create your **KDP** account and an Amazon Author Central account. If people do begin to look, they will find you. Don't expect results quickly. You have to speculate to accumulate. Follow other writers, bloggers and influencers and be the reader/follower/fan you would like to have. Invite people you know are readers to 'like' your page. Share reviews of books you admire, or post links to your own reviews.

Thankfully, you have some time to make friends in the indie playground because now, in spite of my warnings, I suppose you're going to …

4. Write Your Book

For the purposes of this book I'm going to assume that you're a fiction writer, but I quite understand that other genres are popular and viable. Memoirs are big at the moment. People write short stories, self-help books and poetry. All good, and by-and-large my own experiences will still be useful to you if you're going to self-publish.

I write at a PC and I use Word. Other writing programs are available.

I don't presume to tell you how to write your book, but I can give you some insights into how I write mine. I listen in on the conversations of people in cafés. I people-watch. Story suggests itself to me. Often, not the whole story. I might just get a starting point. That's fine. Some writers map out their plots from beginning to end. Some, like me, fly by the seat of their pants and are known in the trade as 'pantsters.' I never know the end of the book from the beginning. Usually I am about 75% through the book before the end comes to me, and it is often a destination I haven't foreseen.

For me, if it isn't too egotistical a thing to claim, writing is almost spiritual. When I am writing, I am lost in something that is bigger than I am. Sometimes, I can't say where the words come from. To create something from literally nothing is supremely satisfying. When I write, I am more 'me' than at any other time.

Ideas have come to me through various means. *Game Show* was the product of being in the audience for a TV game show. *Crossings* had its genus in some wet footprints on a wooden footbridge. *The Hoarder's Widow* developed as a result of viewing—and later buying—a house in which the rooms were so stacked with boxes and junk that it was impossible to see beyond the doorways. *The Cottage on Winter Moss* was inspired by the landscape around where I live. It doesn't matter where your idea comes from, just get one and begin. The first few lines are the most difficult, so stop fussing with your chair, checking social media, playing Solitaire and JUST START.

My methodology is as follows. At the beginning of every new book I imagine that I am a stranger in a new land. I have a safe place to stay and to which I can return if things turn pear-shaped. I look out from that safe place—a blank page—and see, let's say, a road down to a bridge, a path up a hillside, a bus stop. Any of these will take me somewhere in the story. So I pick one. For this example, let's say I choose the road to the bridge. I write that far in the story, describe the view, the times, the weather, maybe introduce a character or two. Then I stop at my metaphorical bridge. Where can I go from here? Is there a path along the river? Is there a car waiting in a lay-by with an interesting driver? Have my characters had a row—do they need to go separate ways? So, the next writing day, I choose one of those options. Or, sometimes, I get to the bridge and find there is nothing, a dead end. If that's so, I retrace my steps (delete delete delete) and go back to the beginning and choose another of the options I had at first.

Every day I write as far as I can see in my story, which is why my books tend to be episodic. I spend the first hour or so going over what I wrote the previous day, honing, improving the language, dithering over semicolons and em dashes, expanding a description here, editing one there. I suppose it is like a sports person's warm up. I have to get back into the groove. Then I shoulder my backpack and set out on the next leg of the journey as far as I can see it.

This strategy has taken me a while to work out. My first book, *Game Show*, took ten years to write. That was partly because I wrote it when I had two small children to take care of, but mainly because I had no clue what I was doing or where I was going. Plus—like many new writers—I wrote secretly. I didn't want to tell anyone what I was up to so naturally I couldn't ask anyone's opinion. When I wasn't writing I was thinking about the book, its characters, its themes. *Game Show* has powerful psychological and political content. It asks why good people do bad things and explores herd mentality. I began with the premise that, given the choice and assured that there would be no negative consequences, most people would do a bad thing rather than a good one. I assumed everyone is inherently bad. But, as I wrote the book, I became less and less sure of that position. Some of my nice, ordinary characters rebelled against the low, selfish things I was asking them to do. Gradually it came to me that rather than being 'good' or 'bad' people are actually just very suggestible, but this was a hunch. I was dealing with things that instinctively I thought were probably true but didn't know for sure. Towards the end of that ten years I came across the work of Dr Philip Zimbardo, whose real-life experiments proved what I had been groping towards. His experiments were well-known in the field of psychology but his book was new. I couldn't have finished *Game Show* without it, so those ten years were necessary in lots of ways.

The main tool of a writer's trade is their imagination and thankfully they can take it everywhere with them. At the risk of not listening to people who are speaking, forgetting why we went into a certain shop, losing track of TV programmes and getting in the way of pedestrians as we stand and stare into space, anywhere and everywhere is a good place to mull over our story. We don't need to be at our desk to be creative and, indeed many times I find that I can be more productive away from mine, picking peas, ironing, walking the dogs. It's all grist to the mill.

So is research. If your book has some technical, historical or scientific basis I urge you to research it thoroughly. Thank heavens for Google! My search history at the end of some days is quite bizarre. What would a prostitute get paid in 1813? How much poppy extract would kill a person? How long would it take to travel from London to Yorkshire by coach in 1835? Writing fiction is all very well but even a novelist can't rewrite the laws of physics or the facts of history and, trust me, some reader out there will see your error and let you know about it. Know your subject, people! I had this powerfully brought home to me when a reader emailed me to let me know I had made a glaring—and very insulting—error about when Canada entered WW2. If there is an advantage to being an indie author and using the various print-on-demand (**POD**) services it is this: it is easy—and fairly instant—to correct your manuscript. As I don't have warehouses of books already printed—blatant errors and-all—I can fix mistakes when I find them. It means that those who have already bought or read the book won't get the best version of it, but at least I can be sure that future readers will.

As I write, some characters invariably inveigle their way into the story without my knowing what they are there for. I let the characters dictate the plot. You get an instinct for these things. Sometimes they lead me down a blind alley but it is my experience that more often than not they know exactly where they are heading. When they do things that surprise me I know I'm on the right lines. It means they are 'alive,' that they have autonomy. That will make them 'real' and relatable to readers. This happened in *Relative Strangers*. It's a book about an extended family which gets together to celebrate a golden wedding anniversary. The family is a mess. Sundry distant members of it keep turning up. I piled the pressure on because I wanted to see what it would take to break that family into pieces. There is one character who is not related in any way to the others. I didn't know what he was for but he would insist on being there. Then, about seventy pages from the end, it came to me, a Eureka moment. There was a role that ONLY he could fill, an essential part, one that would save the rest of the family from itself.

Write *your* book. Trust your instinct as a writer. Call on your knowledge of other books and other writers. Research your subject. Be patient with yourself; writing is a kind of alchemy and these things take time. Strive at all times to make your book the best it can be. Think of it as your child—in a way it is, a creation you have wrought from nothing, given breath and life, flesh and bone, a being you will prepare and send off into the big, wide world to stand or fall on its own merit.

5. 'The End' is only The Beginning

When I have written the words 'the end' I switch off the computer and leave it. I leave it for a week, a month, a year. As exciting as it is to show my baby off, I mustn't. It isn't ready yet. Like a good loaf, it needs to prove. When I go back to it I will see plot holes, character inconsistencies, woolly themes and sloppy writing. There will be things I didn't explain at all, or at all well. There will be other elements that I have done to death. My character's blue eyes will have turned brown. My protagonist will have been in two places at the same time. My tenses will veer from present to past and back again and my point of view will be hopping from one character to another like a flea between dogs. My pacing is too slow, or too fast …

I go back to my book with fresh eyes, ready to question everything about it. I do a Save As and begin work on the second draft. Now that I have the story on the page I can really burrow into my style, language, grammar, point of view, pacing, setting, story arc, my characters' voice ticks and mannerisms, my dialogue, descriptive passages … everything.

I don't worry too much about word count. In my opinion, a book is as long as it needs to be to tell your story. People will tell you that a book more than 70,000 words is too long, but that's rubbish. Look at Hilary Mantel's books, at Margaret Atwood's, at Stephen King's, at Donna Tartt's. Then again, just because it *can* be 250,000 words doesn't mean it *should* be. Are there chapters I can cut out? I routinely ask myself, 'What does this contribute to the story?' If it serves no purpose, I get rid of it.

Once I've completed the second draft, the time might be right to consult a developmental editor, especially if there are areas that I'm unsure of. For much more about editing and the role of the editor, consult Sallianne Hines' book, *About Editing. An essential guide for authors,* a companion volume to this one and a thoroughly useful and easy-to-understand explanation of the whole editing process.

If I can supply a simile here, getting the opinion of a developmental editor is like doing a pregnancy test. Is there something alive in there? Is it viable?

A developmental editor will look at the story arc, the way themes are worked out, style, characters. It will cost money, but the pain of the expense will pale in comparison to the brutal mauling the editor will probably give it. However, there is no gain without pain and, hurtful as it is to get a manuscript back covered in corrections and deletions, the book will undoubtedly be better for it. Plus, if a book has legs, the editor will say so. He or she will be on board—a valuable companion in the onward journey towards publication.

If the budget is zero—but how will you know what the cost might be if you don't at least ask?—one option is to give the precious foetus to a trusted friend to look at. Pick someone who is an avid reader, preferably in the appropriate genre. They should understand what a great privilege it is to read the manuscript. I'd always agree on a time period in which they will read the book and come back with their notes and suggestions. There is nothing worse than being on tenterhooks for a fortnight only to discover that your chosen reader has forgotten all about the manuscript or 'hasn't got round to it yet.' Finally, choose someone who can be trusted to be uncompromisingly honest with you. No one needs a sycophant at this point in the procedure. For this reason it is better to choose someone other than your spouse, parent or child.

This is one place where attempts to make friends in the indie playground pay off. A writer-friend is a reasonable substitute for a professional developmental editor if a professional really cannot be afforded.

Once the manuscript comes back, it takes a couple of weeks to lick the wounds and to assimilate all the feedback, both positive and negative. At the end of the day it's *my* book and I can decide how much of the advice should be incorporated into it.

At this stage it's good motivation to go back and read someone else's book in the light of the editor's or reader's suggestions. Does that book's development/characterisation/style/pace reflect the editor's guidance?

The manuscript is overhauled once more. At this stage the Read Aloud feature of Word is a very useful tool. The voices tend to be somewhat mechanical but following the text on the screen at the same time as having it read out means two senses are engaged with the manuscript. Does the dialogue flow naturally? In particular, repeated words and faulty grammar become obvious.

Give the revision process plenty of time. There is no rush. It needs to stew.

At the point where I begin to make tweaks and additions, only to discover that half a paragraph on I've already put in that exact same phrase or word, it's time to stop.

I'm done.

To give you an idea of time, from beginning to end this process might have taken me between six months and a year. I'm lucky enough to be able to dictate my own timetable, so I can write most days if I want to. Usually I find I can get two or three good, whole writing days into each week. A daily word count of 2000 words is pleasing.

6. Traditional or Self-Publish?

Once the book is in the best shape it can be, it is time to begin thinking about getting it into print; physical, digital or both. If you do want to try the traditional route, now is the time to pursue that goal.

A literary agent will represent you, using their contacts in the publishing industry to get your book in front of editors who are likely to be interested in it. The big, traditional publishing houses will not accept submissions except through an agent. The agent will negotiate terms and make sure any contract is sound. They may also assist you in getting the manuscript you send to them in better shape. After all, it is in their interest as well as yours to ensure that the publishers see the book in its best possible light. Going forward, they will handle matters like translation into different languages and possible film rights. The agent should never charge you anything up front, but will take a percentage of the royalties once the book is placed with a publisher. What's great about having an agent is knowing that they believe in you and your work. They put their reputation on the line by taking you on. It's possible that they may not be able to place the book, but they are ready to spend time and effort on it. Unfortunately, literary agents are extremely difficult to acquire. They are inundated with manuscripts from hopeful writers and can take months or even years to reply. In my experience, lots of them don't reply at all.

A traditional publisher will commit to the book and assign an in-house editor to work on it, alongside you, to further hone the book into shape, ready for the market. This may mean asking you to compromise on plot, style or character if the editor feels that the book would be more marketable—more profitable—in a slightly different guise. The publisher will organise a book cover artist, send **ARC**s (advance review copies) to professional reviewers and critics, plan publicity and your launch. They will have the book printed and distributed to bookshops and also organise its upload in digital format to the various **eBook** platforms. Via their contract with you, they will own the rights to the book.

Generally they will pay an advance as a gesture of goodwill, which could be hundreds or even thousands of pounds/dollars, but you will receive no further royalties until they have recouped their initial outlay. Your contract will specify the percentage of royalties you will receive, which are generally in the area of 5%-12% of wholesale price. So, not much. Many beginners think they are going to 'get rich' with traditional publishing, but this is far from the truth. The traditional publisher may 'option'—that is, get first choice on, your next book.

Some smaller independent traditional publishing houses accept submissions directly from authors. They don't insist on the literary agent as an intermediary. This means you have to be savvy—or take legal advice—about any contract they may supply as you won't have the agent to guide you.

If you later decide to part ways with a publishing house, be aware that the covers they paid for may not be available to you going forward. They may delist the book from online platforms, wiping all the reviews it may have garnered off the slate. The book's copyright must be returned to the author under the terms of the contract but this can sometimes prove difficult. In order to republish the book independently, the author will have to begin from scratch.

No traditional publishing house or reputable agent will *ever* require you to pay them anything, either upfront or after publication. They take their percentage out of the overall earnings.

The benefit of having an agent to represent you or a publisher who accepts your book is that you then have a team of people who are invested—literally and metaphorically—in you and your book. They will assist you in all the ways described above. It sounds marvellous, doesn't it? But then again I hear stories from writers who have been traditionally published and it isn't all plain sailing. Publishing houses are businesses and can insist on changes to your book to make it more marketable, more accessible, to fit it into a popular genre where it may well sell more copies but might not be the book you want it to be. I hear that there isn't much in the way of marketing support and, of course, the author's royalties are less as the publisher wants to recoup all they have outlaid before the writer gets a penny, and only share the royalties thereafter. The bottom line is that everyone involved will want a piece of the pie you have so painstakingly baked, and as a result you may be left with only the crumbs.

Any agent or traditional publisher will take many weeks, or even months, possibly years to respond to you. Some never reply at all. It's a long and largely thankless road. Be prepared.

A vanity press is so-called because it provides the means whereby writers can flatter their own egos, firstly by receiving a fulsomely worded report on their typescript and then by seeing their books in print. A vanity press produces whatever the writer supplies, regardless of its quality or marketability. The author pays 100% of all costs. Vanity publishers have other names for themselves such as subsidy-, self- or cooperative-publishing. Generally, if a publisher is advertising for authors, it is probably a vanity press. Be clear about what your money is buying. Any books produced will remain the property of the press. You may even end up having to buy copies of your own book! You may find you have granted the publishers an exclusive licence to exploit your work. Your fee is for the costs of publication, *not* print. Vanity publishers print copies to order, so claims about the cost of warehousing should be taken with a pinch of salt.

A hybrid publisher is a halfway house between traditional and vanity publishing. Like a traditional publisher, they provide editing, proofreading, marketing, book production and distribution, but the distribution is often just uploading to digital sales platforms, which you can do yourself. Unlike a traditional publisher, they expect the author to share the upfront costs of the process and to share the royalties afterwards. The author gets the benefit of any professionalism and clout the publishing house may have while retaining more control of their book.

A hybrid publisher will have *some* confidence and belief in the book and its author, as they will be making some financial investment, but they have less to lose if sales are disappointing. Both editorial and cover quality is very variable. Personally, I'd be wary. Without knowing exactly what the costs are, how will a writer know that their share is just that—a share—and not in fact the entirety? There are many examples of purportedly hybrid publishers turning out to be vanity publishers in disguise.

Any reputable printworks will print copies of a book from artwork you supply (cover and text), but only in large quantities. If you're confident you can sell your books directly—online and via local outlets and fairs—and you have plenty of storage space for hundreds of paperback or hardcover copies, that might be the way to go, but remember that there will be no opportunity to go back later and correct any errors in the manuscript.

Getting an agent and/or a traditional publisher is a route I have tried and failed, and given up on. If you want to give it a go you might like to visit the websites of traditionally published novelists in your genre to find out which agencies or publishers they are with. Visit the agent's and publisher's websites to see what their submission guidelines are and follow their instructions *to the letter*.

You can Google lists of agents and publishers. Find those who represent your genre.

Alternatively, for a more personal approach, find smaller publishing houses in your area. They may look more favourably on submissions from local writers.

Once again, those on-line writers' groups are a gold mine. Ask the question. Someone out there will know the answer.

Whatever you decide, you are almost certainly going to need a **synopsis** of your novel, probably not more than a couple of hundred words. A synopsis is not a **blurb**. It summarises your story including the plot twists and the surprises you have worked so hard to spin out. It is the hardest thing to write!

You'll also need a query letter to go with your submission. Bear in mind that agents and publishers receive dozens or even hundreds of queries a day. Yours will have to stand out. I was successful in getting an agent back in the old days when you had to send physical submissions through the post. I printed my letter, synopsis and the fifty pages required on bright green paper in the hope that it would stand out from the crowd and, she told me, it worked.

Anything you send to an agent or a publisher must be squeaky clean in terms of grammar and punctuation, concisely written and engaging. If you have an editor, you can ask for their help with your query package.

Self-publishing means exactly that. You publish yourself—with all that entails. But don't despair, that's what this book aims to help you with. You need to wear an author's hat, a publicist's hat and a businessperson's hat, but self-publishing mean means keeping control of your book and reaping 100% of any rewards yourself. It might mean some financial outlay, although it is possible to do the whole thing for free. I don't recommend that, but lots of people do it. I did it myself at first, with fairly miserable results. On the other hand, everyone has to start somewhere. Assuming you're ready to learn a lot, multi-task and wear several hats, let's proceed.

7. The Road to Self-Publishing

After the book has been written and redrafted, and as much of your developmental editor's advice as you can stomach has been taken on board, the book is STILL not finished. It's hard, but resist the temptation to give it out to the people who have expressed an interest in it. Instead, begin to list their names and email addresses. This list is the nucleus of the launch team. We will come back to this in Chapter 11.

At this point one's attention has to split equally between three pathways.

On one path is the book. This is a tortuously winding, backroad of a lane, but one that is still essential to travel. The manuscript needs further honing and improvement as it gets nearer to publication.

On the other path is the publication itself. This is a high-speed dual-carriageway, with a lane for the formatting of the manuscript for upload to the various sales platforms, and another for its launch onto the market.

Note that I refer to **Publication** and **Launch** as two different things.

First I will talk about the book (Chapter 8), and then I'll guide you through the way I format and upload for publication (Chapters 9 & 10). Then we'll deal with orchestrating the launch (Chapter 11).

But I want to emphasise that in terms of time all these pathways need to be trodden at the same time.

See Chapter 12 for a schedule that amalgamates these three pathways.

8. The Book

A. The Alpha Read

Now is the time I share my book with its first non-professional reader. I call this my alpha reader and it is usually my husband. I read the book aloud to him. This is useful in many ways. Reading the book aloud is as essential as hearing it read aloud. Listen to the prose. Is it lilting and musical? Or stark, dramatic and punchy? Or does it drone? Listen to the way the characters' dialogue sounds when spoken out loud. Is it realistic? Does each character have a distinctive 'voice'? Are there repeated words? Suddenly my eyes can spot spelling and grammatical errors my brain has been blind to before reading aloud.

My husband is great at listening attentively, and is not afraid of stopping me when something doesn't make sense—clearly, not adequately explained—or when I have over-egged something. He spots anomalies in plot and character. The viewpoint of a person of the opposite gender is handy, and not one the book has usually enjoyed the benefit of thus far. All kinds of practical questions crop up, such as whether a casserole could have cooked in a specific period of time, how long it actually takes to drive from A to B, if daffodils are likely to still be in evidence at the end of April.

If we are conscientious about it, we can usually get through the book in about a week. I make notes as I go along, careful not to let any suggestion for improvement slip past me.

If you don't have a partner or friend who will allow you to read the book aloud to them and who you can trust to be *constructively* critical, approach one of your new indie friends. What you're looking for at this stage is a guineapig reader who is prepared to read the book slowly and analyse it deeply, and then discuss it with you in minute detail. For this reason a person you can connect with face-to-face is going to be better than someone with whom you only have a social media relationship.

There is something quite momentous about the alpha read. If having a developmental edit is like doing a pregnancy test, the alpha read is like the third trimester ultrasound scan. The baby is fully formed and can be sexed. It's complete. It's even viable—just about—but it needs time to grow, to mature, to get strong. Everything you do from now on will be about bringing the being within you to perfection, and introducing it to the world.

Once the alpha read is done, go back to the manuscript to make all the corrections, additions and deletions required. It might need an extra chapter or two where the alpha reader feels the plot has not unfurled seamlessly. On the other hand, it might mean deleting episodes that have led the reader astray or not made a strong enough contribution to character or plot.

B. The Beta Read

Approach two trusted indie friends and request them to beta read the book. A beta read is a thorough, critical read-through of the book, much like an alpha read but the issues raised by your alpha reader will already have been addressed. This process is all about fine-tuning—perfecting every little detail. Everything is on the table, from plot, pacing, character, language, to possible triggers and questions of sensitivity. If there are aspects of the book that might be sensitive—race, religion, disability, sexuality, gender—I will at this time also approach a **sensitivity reader,** someone who is experienced or expert in that field. I recommend Deirdre O'Grady at www.abilitywise.ie for any books that include disability or characters with learning differences. She is also very helpful with aspects of mental health and addiction.

Again, having a pool of contacts is essential here. I've reached out twice on a popular on-line book group for experts in disability and rehabilitation, and been lucky enough to enlist the help of two wonderful women, experienced and highly qualified in their fields. For *The Lady in the Veil*, which includes a character of colour, I approached my local branch of an anti-racist group and found a sensitivity reader who helped me out in return for a donation.

I tell my readers what areas I'm concerned about so that they can give me specific feedback, but other than that I allow them to approach the book as any ordinary reader would. It's best to agree on a timescale so that they know how long they have got. In addition, it limits the length of time I have to be on tenterhooks. I'd say a fortnight is reasonable, but of course we have to be flexible.

Meanwhile, this is no time for resting on the laurels. There is other work to be done.

C. Begin to Assemble a Launch Team
See Chapter 11.

D. Think About the Book Cover

I'm told a book cover has less than three seconds to engage a potential reader's interest, so it's important to get it right. In those three seconds the cover has to engage the interest of a potential reader and convince them that they can trust what is presented there sufficiently to risk investigating further.

KDP (Kindle Direct Publishing) provides some templates and stock images for book covers and in the beginning I did use them, but to be honest they can be spotted a mile off and immediately set off readers' shoddy-cover-shoddy-book sensors.

You could look at current trends in book covers to see if you could emulate those, or search other books in your genre but be careful not to copy. Book covers are copyrighted just like book contents.

Things to consider very carefully are the image that will dominate the page, the font type, size and spacing, the colour palette. All of these must of course reflect the book's content. A cover with an iridescent dragon might be very appealing, but if your book is about life in a convent it might be called misleading. Make sure your cover looks good as a small thumbnail as well as in full size. Remember that the thumbnail image on a screen is going to be most people's first view of it. Make sure that the cover is going to be right for your genre.

It's possible to design your own cover with your own artwork or photograph. You CAN'T just take images off the internet and hope no one notices. Personally, I use local artists to create original artwork. Generally they are delighted to be asked, and provide artwork at a reasonable or even at no cost. Naturally they get the credit within the book. If they have galleries or websites they sometimes buy copies of the book to sell. Visiting local art groups or art colleges might be a good start. Professional cover designers are available, of course, and if there's money in the budget they are quick and efficient people to deal with. Some have a stock of ready-to-go covers they can adapt with your title. Again, the on-line writers' groups are a mine of useful contacts.

Whichever route is taken it is important to give the designer a good brief, show examples of the styles of cover you like, suggest a colour palette and even provide photographs. However, I've found that when working with artists it's important to allow their artistic instinct some input too. Coming up with good covers has been one of the most difficult aspects of the whole business for me. Usually I know what I want but my drawing skills are nil. I have no option but to allow someone else's involvement. It's a bit like taking your toddler for his first haircut. Some other hand will, for the first time, have an effect on the way he looks. I can't be the only mother who cried in the hairdressers while their child sat in the chair. I know I still have a lock of hair that I jealously collected from the floor. The best counsel I can give is, having selected your artist or graphic designer, trust them.

Once the cover image is decided (and why not use the launch team to bounce different ideas off?) you will need to create a print-ready PDF but this won't be possible until you have formatted your book—that is, establish what size it will be, and how many pages. I use a local graphic designer to do this for me but if you're savvy at desktop publishing, you can probably do this yourself. KDP provides a template based on your book's size. We will explore this in Chapter 9 Section B point xxvi.

If you intend to publish both a print and a **Kindle**—digital—version of the book, you'll need two cover versions of the same design. One will be a simple front cover image, which should be a print-ready .jpeg file of a minimum dpi of 300 in RGB format. The second will be a high-resolution full cover spread, with front, spine and back, saved as a PDF in CMYK format. Don't ask me what all that means, I just know that's what you need!

E. Search for an Editor

If there is no budget for anything else, finding the fee for a professional editor is the one thing I wouldn't compromise on, even if I have to use my holiday fund, birthday and Christmas money to pay for it.

There are so many self-published books out there that are poorly edited, full of typos and grammatical errors, sloppily written with meandering story arcs. Please, please, don't add to the swamp.

Indie writers have had a bad reputation and it only takes one reviewer to comment on poor editing to give a book the kiss of death. Getting a professional editor on board has been the best move I ever made. Get recommendations from other writers (here's mine: www.quinnediting.com) but do ensure that the editor is well-versed in your genre. For much more on editing and its importance I recommend Sallianne Hines' book, *About Editing. An essential guide for authors.* This book explains in layman's terms the various kinds of editing and editors available. Initially, the editor will want to know the genre of your book, its length, and what you're looking for from them. Discuss timing and, of course, the cost. Many editors will do a sample edit for you free of charge. Take advantage of this and pick the one who responds quickly and who feels most in tune with your work. This may well be the person who did your developmental edit (assuming you paid a professional) but may not be.

Alternatively, if you really *really* cannot afford to pay, there are programs you can buy which will help you identify spelling and grammar errors. Grammarly is one I know of, but have never used. ProWritingAid is another. Wordtune is free. It seems to me, though, that a computer programme is not going to be well-equipped to judge lyrical prose or the nuances of everyday speech. Better then to find a person who is an English teacher, a journalist, a librarian or someone with excellent credentials in the language. Editing is a professional skill and requires concentration and attention to detail. It's too easy to get swept up in the story and not notice the glaring errors but a professional editor has learned to resist that temptation.

I have a BA and an MA in English but I'm blind to my errors when it comes to my own writing. The writer is the worst possible person to edit their own work.

F. Commission the Editor
Once the book comes back from the beta readers it's time to assimilate their feedback. As with the developmental editor, it can be hard to take any criticism but I want the book to be the best iteration of itself that it can be, and I asked those readers for input because I respected their opinions.

In particular the feedback of the sensitivity reader is especially important. The world of political correctness can be a minefield these days. I was encouraged to create ethnically diverse characters after the murder by the police of George Floyd. The Black Lives Matter campaign really began to find its voice and the world of literature was, quite rightly, challenged to be much more inclusive. However, a counter reaction then ensued in which ethnic minority writers began to insist that *only they* could authentically render the mindset and experiences of ethnic minority characters. It was at this point that the role of the sensitivity reader became crucial. Unfortunately, some people saw it as an opportunity to make money and the fees charged were, in my view, extortionate. Thankfully, some sensitivity readers offered their services as a genuine attempt to make fiction more inclusive. Sensitivity for issues of race was soon followed—again, quite rightly—by a call for more inclusivity for the disabled, the neuro-diverse and the LGBTQ+ community. I try to be much more inclusive in my writing these days, not to tick a box or to ride a bandwagon but because I want my books to be a more authentic reflection of the world I see around me.

I make any changes suggested by the beta team to the manuscript and save it twice, first as a Master copy with the date, and then again as the copy to send to the editor. Less ruthless than a developmental edit, a line or copy editor will get deeply into the nitty-gritty of the book, fine-tuning the prose, correcting spelling and grammar and challenging the style. They will identify the obstacles that readers will encounter in terms of believable and relatable characters, confused time-lines, flimsy motives and so on. What they will not do is challenge the overarching concept of the book. We are way past that point. They will tweak, they will not hack.

My editor is American. As the majority of my readers are American, she helps me ensure that they will understand my very British books. We have endless fun email exchanges about what an American reader's idea of a purse is, as opposed to what I mean by it.

Once more, just because the book is out of your hands for a while does not mean you do not have work to do. While the editor is busy it's time for you to

G. Write the Blurb

The term **Blurb** is a *bona fides* writing and publishing expression and refers to the short, enticing description that appears on the back of a print book, on the book's sales page or in a query letter to an agent. Like the synopsis, it is terribly tricky to write. It needs to be short—certainly no longer than 250 words—punchy and intriguing, inviting potential readers into the story without giving too much away.

Think if the blurb as a movie trailer rather than a product description. Use short, catchy sentences that are easy to read, and arrange the text in well-spaced paragraphs rather than one block of text.

Now that you have at least three people on the team who have read the book (the one alpha and the two beta readers) it's possible to bounce ideas off them. Quite often I find they are willing or even itching to have a go at writing the blurb themselves. If your book contains themes or incidents that might be **triggers** for some readers—alcoholism, domestic violence, rape, drug use, for instance—you should include a trigger-warning in your blurb.

It is worth having expanded and contracted versions of your blurb. Different platforms require different wordcounts so do the work now. Also, when you come to promoting your book, some companies allow only 350 characters, so be ready to distil your blurb right down to its bare bones.

Once you have a draft version of the blurb, share it with your launch team to see what they think. Based on the blurb, would they buy the book? Be ready for twenty different opinions, but if nothing else, this process serves to whet the appetite of the team as their investment in the project is crucial to a successful launch.

H. Create Your Final Draft

Once the editor has finished their work, you will need to amend and correct your manuscript, adding in or deleting as appropriate. Most editors use Word's Track Changes. You might choose to Accept—or Reject—the amendments and corrections suggested, or you can do what I do, which is to transfer them one by one into my own copy. I find this method makes me really think about each suggested alteration, rather than automatically just accepting them. Don't be dismayed by the amount of errors highlighted, or the number of changes suggested. Of course, this is your book and you don't have to incorporate all the suggested edits, but you'd be mad not to correct the spelling and grammatical mistakes at the very least, otherwise what was the point in commissioning the editor?

Finally, get someone to proofread the book, to iron out those last, tiny glitches. Your editor might do this for you, for an additional fee, or you might include it in the original contract.

Save this document as a Master and date it so that you know that, going forward, you are using the beautifully edited, corrected manuscript.

I. Send the ARC (Advance Review Copy) to the Launch Team and Book Bloggers

The end result of the alpha and beta reads, the sensitivity read, the editing and the proofreading is one Master document that incorporates all suggestions and corrections. This, the final draft, now becomes the Advance Review Copy of the book to be sent out to the launch team. At last, your baby is ready to be born, at least into the pure and rarefied atmosphere of the birthing suite. It may not be quite perfect. You can trust your launch team—your midwives—to identify any small issues and help you put them right.

Most people will read the ARC on their Kindles and to do this they will need a file called an **.ePub**, which you can make as follows.

Either: download a free programme called Calibre, upload your final draft into it and get it to convert to an .ePub. Calibre is free but the folks there need to eat, so it would be nice if you made a financial contribution.

Or: flick forward to Chapter 9 Section C, Point iv to see how **Kindle Create**—another free program—can make an .ePub for you. Nowadays, as I've given in to using Kindle Create to format my eBooks, I use this option.

Either way, make an .ePub file of your book and send it to your launch team. See Chapter 11 Sections A and B for more details.

The month or so I allow my team to read and write a review for the book is a busy time for me. Not only am I removing the tumbleweeds of fluff and debris that have accumulated in the house while I have been busy writing the book, and locating my husband underneath the avalanche of laundry that has amassed, but I also use the time to tackle the formatting and to begin the process of uploading the book to the various sales platforms.

Necessarily, because the launch team will find glitches and typos, this can only be quite tentative. My ARC isn't ready to become my published book until I'm sure it's perfect. However, it is possible to format the book and upload it without hitting the Publish button and as formatting can be a time-consuming and frustrating process, I begin it early. Formatting can be hired out, of course, so check those online groups for recommendations. Some editors also format. Ask yours.

9. Formatting for Upload to KDP (Kindle Direct Publishing)

If you choose to format your own manuscript, read on.

What I mean by formatting is getting your manuscript into the right formats for KDP's publishing platform in both print and eBook formats, and then uploading them. Formatting for eBook format is easy. I'm going to show you how to do that using Kindle Create. Formatting for print is more difficult but we will come to it in due course.

Formatting is the part of the job I least enjoy because every platform seems to want something slightly different and there is a formatting gremlin that seems to take delight in making my PDFs and .ePubs somehow not quite right. Plus, every time you create the manuscript in a different format, things within it seem to alter. It has to be checked, checked and checked again. It is time-consuming and laborious, but it has to be done.

To reiterate, I work on the formatting whilst the launch team are working on the ARC. I constantly remind myself that the manuscript will *still* be subject to alterations. Unless I'm submitting the eBook for **pre-order**, I only ever save it on the publication platform as Draft, holding back on hitting the Publish button until I'm certain that I'm ready.

A. Add front and backmatter

Firstly, to the final, dated Master document you saved and sent to the launch team in Chapter 8 Point I, if you have not done so already, add:

i. A title page and
ii. A copyright page. This doesn't need to be complicated or legally registered anywhere. It simply states that the material is copyrighted and identifies you as the owner of it. My copyright page says: © *Allie Cresswell, 2023. Except as provided by the Copyright Act [1956, 1988, 2003] no part of this publication may be reproduced, stored in a retrieval system or transmitted in any*

form or by any means without the prior written permission of the publisher.

Allie Cresswell asserts her moral rights to be identified as the author of this work.

This is a work of fiction; no similarity to any real person or persons is intended or should be inferred.

Some writers like to register their copyright so that they have legal proof of ownership of it in case of plagiarism or copyright infringement. This is an option, but not required by law.

iii. Add a dedication if you are using one,

iv. Plus any other front-matter you wish to include, such as a quote from a poem or similar, so long as you have permission to do so.

v. Ensure each chapter will begin on a new page and the chapter headings are formatted in Styles Sheet as Headings. This will be important later.

vi. At the end of the document, called back matter, I include a short paragraph inviting readers to review the book and explaining why this is important to me. I recommend you do the same.

vii. I also add a short bio with a picture, and mention my Facebook, Twitter and Instagram handles and my website address. It's up to you if you wish to do likewise.

viii. Always include a bibliography if you have used reference books more than just in passing.

ix. I list my other published books.

x. Sometimes I add questions for reading groups.

xi. Never, ever, in any of these elements do I have anything in Times New Roman font. I don't know why, but if the PDF version includes even so much as a full stop in **TNR** it will be rejected.

xii. Save As. I call this document Master doc for eBook and I add the date because this document will supersede all other versions of it and I want to be sure of ALWAYS working with the correct, most recent version. This is an A4 format (8.5 x 11in) document with normal margins, line-spaced at 1.5. I use Garamond as my main body text font and sometimes another font (but never Times New Roman) for chapter headings etc. This document will be the basis for the e-reader versions of the book. Leave that to one side for now.

B. Prepare and Upload Your Book for its PRINT version
You might like to tick off each step as you complete it.

i. Next, I return to my Master document and do another Save As, this time naming the file Master doc for Print, again adding the date. Use this document to format for the physical print version of the book, as follows:

ii. Use the Word Style Sheets to decide on typefaces for your text and chapter headings, footnotes—if any—and front and back matter. Choose text size. I use 12pt.

iii. Use the Paragraph tab to decide on indents, linespacing and so forth. If in doubt, pick up a paperback or hardback book and see how it has been formatted.
Usually, fiction books should have indented paragraphs and no extra space between paragraphs. Nonfiction books do not need indents and can have extra spacing between paragraphs, OR they can follow the style of fiction. Memoirs can also choose a fiction or a nonfiction style.

Linespacing is the space between lines of text, and can vary from 1 point to more. Double spacing of a 12-point typeface would be 24 points. Personally, I space at 1.5 on my 12-point text, so that's 18 points. Nonfiction or memoir books can be set more closely.

Neglecting these details is an immediate clue that a book has not been traditionally published, and could prejudice readers who have been caught in the swamp of poorly formatted and edited self-published books in the past.

Make sure you have use Insert New Page at the end of each chapter. Don't use lots of Returns.

iv. Go to the Layout tab of the Word document and then open up the Page Setup section. Here the page size, margins and the **gutter** (the white space between the type and where the pages meet the spine) can be adjusted to make sure that your book's print area will be correct when you upload it. The gutter allows for the extra thickness of the book created by the book binding. I use KDP's 6 x 9in format for my books but other size options are available. Check which one you want to use. The margins and gutter can be a matter of trial and error and much will depend on how many pages your book is. The more pages, the bigger the gutter. Below you will see my layout for *The Widow's Weeds*, which is a 400-page book. For readers in the US, you can choose inches rather than centimetres.

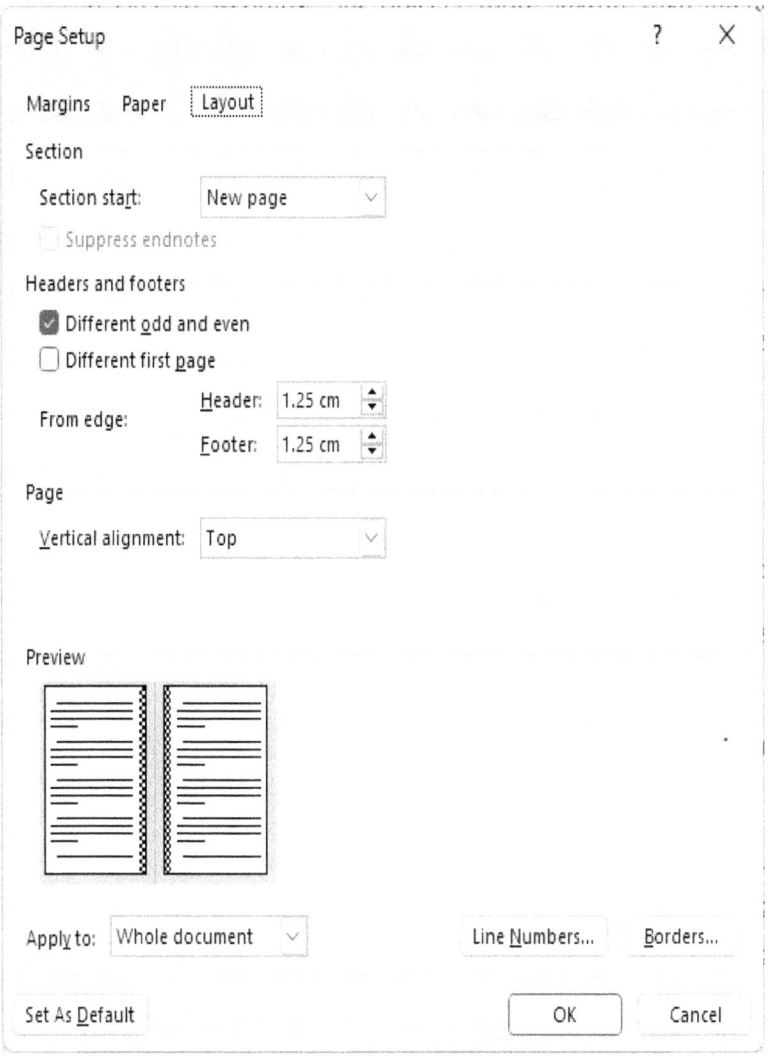

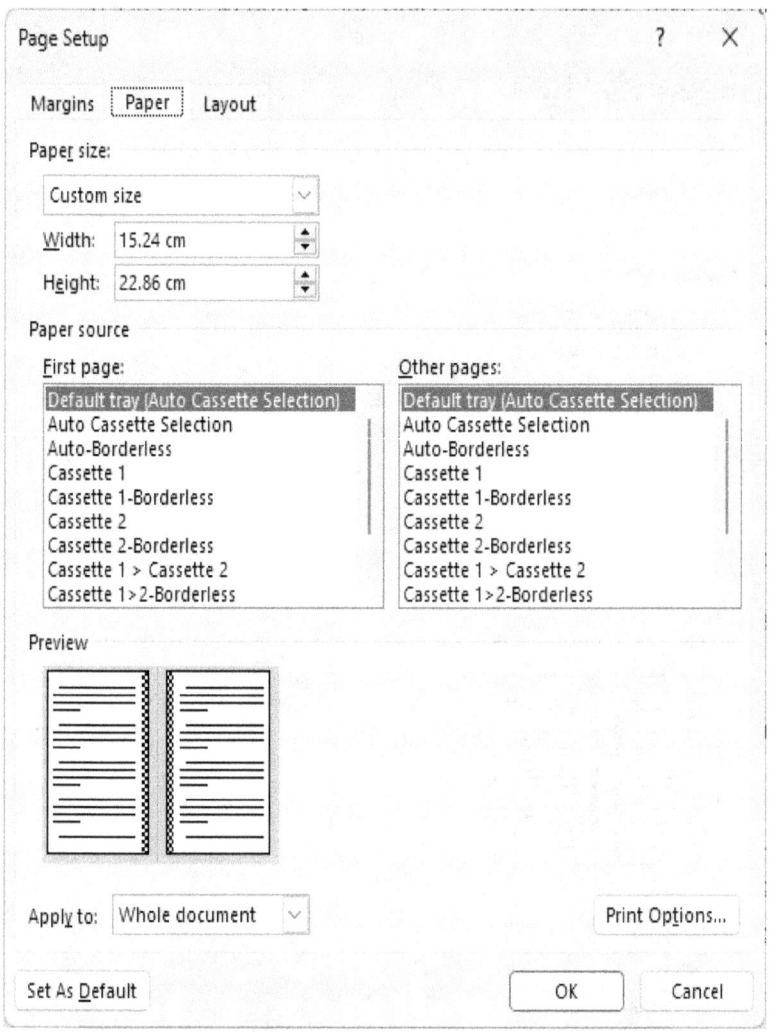

v. Inevitably, making these alterations will throw other things out, so scroll through the manuscript and make sure that there are no extra blank pages and that chapters all begin at the top of the page.

vi. Ensure the title page and dedication, plus other front-matter pages appear on the right-hand pages. Paperback books should always have the title on the first right-hand page, the copyright details on the back of that page, then the dedication and any other information should always be on a right-hand page. You may need to insert blank pages to ensure this falls correctly. Some writers like each new chapter to begin on a new right-hand page but this may well add to your page count which will in turn add to the cost of the book's production. I compromise by having each new chapter begin on a new page but not necessarily a right-hand one.

vii.   Insert page numbers.

viii. Add a Contents page if you're brave enough and if you think the book really needs one. Non-fiction books generally do, fiction books generally don't. This book will. I'll have to gird my loins for that ordeal! Be sure that the page numbers for each chapter as shown on the contents page are correct, and be ready to go back and check they're STILL correct after you make any changes.

ix.   Unfortunately the only way to see if you've got the print area and gutter size right is to upload it to KDP and see, so that's what needs to be done next. We'll take it slowly, step by step.

I strongly suggest you read through the points below to make sure you have the answers to all the questions to hand before you attempt it. Most things can be changed afterwards but the title and subtitle can *not* be changed so be very sure you have those right. Some of the fields—such as keywords—will need some research ahead of time. Write your answers down so that you can easily transfer them when you're ready and so that you can refer back to them when you upload your eBook and upload to other platforms.

You are going to need an **ISBN** number as part of this process. Buy that—or those—now, from Nielson in the

UK or Bowker in the US. I strongly urge you to buy your own ISBN rather than using the free one KDP will offer. Using their ISBN will identify THEM as the publisher of your book and not you, and causes issues down the line if you choose to go wide, that is, publish on platforms other than KDP. A separate ISBN is needed for each different version of your book: eBook, paperback, hardback and audio, and for large print versions of paperback and hardback. You don't have to tell Nielson or Bowker anything about the book that the ISBN will be used for. I buy ISBNs about twenty at a time and register myself as the publisher.

x. Save the newly formatted and dated Master doc for print and then Save As again but this time save it as Print Placeholder, as a reminder that this is NOT the final version and SHOULD NOT be published.

xi. Go to KDP. If you have not opened an account there, do this first. Then choose Create and select the paperback option. The next screen is the paperback details section, also called **metadata**, and requires filling in as follows:

xii. Language. English in my case.

xiii. Book title and subtitle (if required) Many books have phrases like 'A heart-rending romance,' or 'Thrilling and Suspenseful' as their subtitles. Personally, there's nothing that annoys me more than being told how a book will make me feel. That's for me to decide. However, here, you can choose, but be very sure about what you enter into these title and subtitle fields as it can't be changed afterwards. *Think* about it carefully. Don't do it by the seat of your pants.

xiv. Series. If the book is in a series, like *The Talbot Saga,* here is where that is established. If you're not sure whether your book will have sequels, I'd leave this blank. You can always go back to it at a later date.

xv. Edition number. This is for books that have been previously published but that have been substantially overhauled. If this is a new book, leave it blank.

xvi. Author and other contributors. Me. Other contributors are those who have made substantial contributions, such as the editor of an anthology or the artist of an illustrated book. Editors, alpha and beta readers do *not* go here.

xvii. Description. The book's blurb, see Chapter 8 Section G.

xviii. Publishing rights. This is explained on the screen. I always choose 'I own the copyright.'

xix. Keywords. These are the words or phrases that someone might use in searching for a book like this one. For this book I might use: self-publishing; how to self-publish; indie publishing; book launch; how to launch a book; self-publishing success. There is a programme called Publisher Rocket that helps you search for keywords. Lots of writers swear by the importance of keywords but I'm ambivalent about them as I would rarely search for a book in that way. The keywords don't have to be single words, you can use phrases such as genre-types (sweet clean romance), themes (resilience of the human spirit), topics (divorce and remarriage) and settings (books set in Yorkshire). Do the legwork beforehand. Go to Amazon and enter search terms someone might use in looking for a book like yours, and see what comes up.

xx. Categories. Clicking on the Choose Categories button allows the choice of two categories where the book sits most comfortably and to its best effect. This is where your book will succeed or fail in getting a good ranking. Unfortunately the categories are quite broad so you have to choose the best fit. If it fits into a niche, all the better. The smaller the category the less the competition for ranking. However, you have to be reasonable. I once saw a Jane Austen variation that was top in its category, but its category was 'roofing and guttering!' Look up the books in your genre that you feel your book sits most comfortably beside. What categories are they in?

xxi. Adult Content. A pornographic or erotic book, or one containing graphic violence must be declared as such.

Save, and continue to the paperback content section.

xxii. ISBN. Here is where you enter the ISBN you bought at stage ix.

xxiii. Publication date. Leave that blank. KDP does not allow pre-orders for print books. The book will be published the day you hit Publish My Book. We're not ready for that yet.

xxiv. Print options. Choose what paper colour you want. There is a choice of two: cream or white. Traditionally, fiction uses cream and non-fiction uses white. Choose whether the text will be single colour (black ink on the cream or white paper) or choose full colour if the book has colour illustrations. Choose the trim size. Mine are 6 x 9 in. Choose the cover option, matt or glossy. Establish what is typical for your genre by comparing your book with similar ones.

xxv. Manuscript. Here is where to upload the Placeholder Print document you made at step ix. A Word document is fine at this stage. Remember, this is just a vehicle to assist you in getting the margins and gutters of your document correct.

xxvi. Unfortunately, KDP won't allow you to use their Print Previewer function to check your margins and gutters until you also upload a cover file, which you will not have ready yet because the trim size and number of pagers isn't yet established. For now, choose the Cover Create option and use one of KDP's cover options to hash together a Placeholder cover, just temporarily.

xxvii. Now, with a Placeholder manuscript and a temporary cover, you can use the Print Previewer button to see how your margins and gutters are looking. Is the print area fully utilised? You don't want huge gaps at either side as this is inefficient, making your book more pages than it needs to be, thus increasing production costs and reducing profit margin. Also, it won't look professional. The pane on the left should advise you as to optimum margin and gutter sizes for your book. Even so, be prepared to adjust margins and gutters on your Placeholder document and re-upload several times. Only when you're happy, transfer the final dimensions to the dated Master Print document.

xxviii. While you are on this screen, you can download a cover template to your PC.

xxix. To do this, click on the Download a KDP Template link in the Book Cover section. This will allow you to create a template based on your book's page count and the trim size you have chosen, which you can use for the formatting of the print cover, as suggested in Chapter 8 Section D.

xxx.   Download the template to your PC and use it to make your own cover, or send it to your cover designer, adding the cover image, title and so on you've fixed on. Many professional cover designers already have the KDP templates for all trim sizes and page numbers.

xxxi.   Save on KDP as Draft. This is as far as you need to progress at this point. The purpose of steps xxii through to xxx is to establish the margins and gutter size for the print book and to get a template for the cover, both of which you now have.

xxxii.   Once you have the high-resolution print-ready PDF cover made to the specifications of the template in CMYK colour, upload it. Now you can hit Print Previewer to see how the cover looks.

xxxiii.   Save as draft. Don't be tempted to progress further yet. As your launch team provides you with any tiny corrections, incorporate them into the dated Master Print and dated Master eBook Word documents. Once complete, these will be the very final, most perfect version of your book. I save them in a new Files for Publication folder where I also store my print-ready cover PDF and other files, of which more later. Now you can proceed to complete and upload your perfect, error-free book for its print version by converting your Word document into a PDF.

xxxiv.   Check that your fonts are **embedded** in your final, dated, Master Print document by clicking File in Word, then Options then Save. Ensure that Embed Fonts in the File is checked, and that the two boxes beneath, Embed Only the Characters and Do Not Embed Common System Fonts are both unchecked. Then hit OK.

xxxv.   Ensure the dimensions for margins and gutter size have been transferred from the Placeholder document into the dated Master Print file. The placeholder file can now be discarded. Scroll through the document one more time to make sure there are no blank pages, that chapters all begin at the top of the page, that the front matter is arranged properly, that the contents page, if you are using one, shows the correct page numbers. Are you happy with the fonts you've chosen for the title and chapter headings? Are illustrations—if any—the correct size and properly aligned on the page?

xxxvi. Save your dated Master Print document as a PDF. This means the lovely fonts you have picked for your print book will be faithfully reproduced. Check for Times New Roman by going to File in the PDF and then selecting Properties. Scroll down the font list. If TNR is mentioned, it will not be embedded and will not pass muster later, but if you have embedded your non-TNR fonts as above, you should be OK.

xxxvii. Return to KDP and upload your final, dated, Master, PDF. Use the print previewer to make sure the book looks as you wish: the margins and gutter are correct, there are no blank pages and (if you have used one) your contents page shows all the correct page numbers.

xxxviii. Save and proceed to the final paperback rights & pricing screen. Once again, I suggest you read through the next steps ahead of time and make sure you've researched all the fields so you've got the information to hand. For instance, you should research pricing of comparable books.

xxxix. Territories. Check the box that applies.

xl. Primary marketplace. For me, this is the US as I sell most of my books there.

xli. Pricing, royalty and distribution. I suggest you do some research to see what other authors you can reasonably compare yourself with are charging for their print books. Don't be greedy, but don't sell yourself too cheaply either. What do you consider a reasonable—and realistic—return per book for your hard work? Determine on your price and put it into the box. The programme will calculate your royalties. You can allow KDP to calculate the prices in all countries based on your primary marketplace price, or you can decide these yourself. For example, I always charge a little less in the UK and a little more in the EU than suggested. It is recommended that prices always end in .99 or .49 in every currency.

xlii. Expanded distribution. If you only intend to list your book on KDP you should check this box. It means that your book will be available to independent and high street book retailers to buy, but your royalty rate will be reduced for these 'trade' sales in comparison to 'retail' sales via Amazon stores. However, in reality, few book shops are happy to buy from their biggest competitor, so you may not find your book in your local book shop if you go down this route. Increasingly, I don't use Amazon's expanded distribution because I **'go wide.'** More of this in Chapter 10.

xliii. Now, at last, if you're ready, hit Publish Your Book. If you're unsure about the timing, refer to the schedule in Chapter 12. Hurrah! You're done—with this section, anyway! Congratulations. If you're not ready, for instance if you feel that your manuscript is not error-free, Save as Draft.

C. **Prepare and upload your book for its E-READER (Kindle) version**

   i. Return to the dated Master doc for eBook you made at Section B point i of Chapter 9.

ii. Ensure this has been updated with corrections mentioned by the launch team as they read the ARC and is identical to your Master Print document in terms of its content. This document does not need page numbers or the extra pages you inserted for the print version. A plain A4 format (8.5 x 11in) with normal margins will be fine.

iii. You can use this document to upload directly to KDP if you wish, but their preferred format is a **.KPF** file you will create using their free Kindle Create programme. I've fought it for a long time, as Kindle Create has such a limited selection of fonts for chapter headings and the like, but the truth is that Kindle Create will make a .KPF (Kindle package file) that provides the functionality that Kindle e-readers require, such as the Go To menu, which allows readers to flip from one chapter to another, make notes, highlight passages and so on. This functionality is partly enabled by the way you formatted your chapter titles as Headings, as mentioned in Chapter 9 Section A. It makes for a better reading experience for the user, so, reluctantly, I've given in to it.
Alternatively, you can make a PDF document of your Master eBook and use another free programme called Calibre to make an .ePub.

iv. Download the free Kindle Create programme.

v. Click Create New and then Choose. On the next screen, chose your dated Master eBook file.

vi. Once you've hit Let's Get Started, choose from Themes—a woeful selection of three at this point.

vii. Select *your* chapter headings from the pane on the left. Kindle Create errs on the side of caution and chooses lots of potential headings including the title and copyright pages that aren't chapters. Just check those that will facilitate the book's functionality for Kindle readers, such as your chapters, acknowledgements and so on. As a rule of thumb, if you have formatted a title or heading in your dated Master eBook File, then it should be checked here.

viii. Now scroll through the manuscript within the Kindle Create programme, setting and formatting the chapter headings, sub-headings and so on by using the options on the right. It is fairly easy, even if not very satisfactory if you wanted a certain funky or designer look to your eBook.

ix. When you're done, click Review to see how your book looks on the small screen. If you're happy, save and then Export your eBook.

x. You can now choose to export your book in two formats, the .KPF format and also an .ePub format. Choose both, giving a name and a date that will instantly help you to identify them. Make sure you look to see which file on your PC they've been saved in. I add these to my new Files for Publication folder. Why .ePub as well as .KPF? Because KDP will require the .KPF file whilst other platforms require the .ePub file. Whichever way you produce your .ePub file, be sure to review it carefully to make sure it looks as you wish it to look, with no blank pages, consistent font sizes and so on. My PC doesn't open .ePubs so I have to send it to my Kindle, or use Kindle Create's previewer. Calibre also has a previewer function.

xi. You can use the .ePub to send to your launch team. See Chapter 8 Section I and also Chapter 11 Section B.

xii. To an extent your Master eBook Word file is now redundant, as you can make small changes to the manuscript within Kindle Create using the Find function. However, I do always keep it updated along with the Master Print file, just in case.

xiii. You're now ready to upload the digital (eReader) version of your book to KDP.

xiv. Return to the KDP bookshelf where the print book should already be, either published or in draft, on your bookshelf. Choose Create Kindle eBook. Again, read through the points below to make sure you have all the information you're going to need. Some of it will replicate the details you used for the print version of the book, but some will be new. Hopefully you wrote your answers down as suggested.

xv. Input your book's details. You're an old hand at this now. If you wish, you can choose entirely different keywords and put this version of your book into different categories. The categories you are offered are different here in eBooks. Did you look up comparable books to see how their eBook versions were categorised?

xvi. Pre-order. I do use this function nowadays because I'm lucky enough to have people looking out for my new releases, and Amazon will kindly let readers who have read my other books know that a new one is pending. Whilst in pre-order, the manuscript can still be amended (by uploading new files) up to about five days before the book is finally released. Even for entirely debut authors, although numbers of pre-orders are likely to be few, I'd suggest it is useful to set a pre-order purely because it will provide a **purchase link** if you haven't time to publish the print version quietly ahead

	of time or if you've decided to publish only as an eBook. If you're going to have a blog tour, you'll need to supply a purchase link. See Chapter 11 Section A.
xvii.	Save and continue to the next screen. Here you can upload your .KPF or .ePub file and also your simple front cover image file. Go back to Chapter 8, Section D to remind you of the file format you need.
xviii.	Use the previewer to make sure your book looks as you wish.
xix.	eBooks are not required by Amazon to have an ISBN but other platforms do require one. If you plan to publish on other platforms, add your own ISBN, which must be different from the one you used for your print book.
xx.	Save and continue to the next screen, where you can choose to enrol your book in Kindle Unlimited (**KU**) if you wish. Kindle Unlimited is a subscription service offered by Amazon, in which readers pay an amount each month and are allowed to download a quantity of enrolled books free of charge. The author gets paid nothing until the books are read, and then we are paid so much per page. I have some of my books enrolled with KU as a way of engaging readers in the hope that they will go on to buy other books. If you're writing a series, you could enrol just the first book, but members of KU tend to 'buy' books quite rarely, in the same way that subscribers to Netflix tend only to watch the films covered by their subscription; why would they pay twice? You can enrol your book for three months but you must remember to go back and uncheck the box that will keep on signing you up. If you write in a popular 'budget' genre, such as romance or crime, I'd suggest giving KU a try. If you write literary fiction or highbrow books for 'business class' readers, I'd suggest your target audience are not members of KU. Note that

if you sign up for KU you *must not* publish your eBook on any other platform. It is locked exclusively to KDP for a minimum of three months.

xxi. The rest of this screen is the same as the one you filled in for the print book. Again, as regards pricing, look to see what your competitors are asking for their books. Some authors charge 99p/c for their books but personally, I think that's too cheap to be sustainable. And cheap things have small worth. Readers may not value a book they bought for next to nothing.

i. Once the launch team has let you know of any glitches and you have made the necessary corrections within the Kindle Create file and re-uploaded the .KPF or .ePub—sometimes several times until you're quite sure your manuscript is perfect—then you're ready to hit Publish. If you chose Pre-order you must submit your final files five days before the release date.

10. Going Wide

Going Wide is industry slang for selling a book on platforms other than, or in addition to, KDP. Amazon is huge and should certainly be given the credit for pioneering the way for authors to publish their books independently. It must be the biggest global retailer on the planet and I'm sure it sells more books than high street booksellers. There can't be many people who do not have an Amazon account. It is most people's go-to place to buy almost everything. Therefore, as people with a product to sell, we cannot afford to ignore it.

Then again, for the very reason that it is so dominant, some people boycott it, preferring to buy local and to use small shops, including online ones. These consumers are a small but vociferous force in the marketplace and it is not sensible to exclude them from a marketing plan.

Likewise, in these cash-strapped times, many readers still use libraries.

Although it is possible for small book sellers and libraries to buy books from Amazon, in reality it doesn't happen very often. There is a general reluctance by them to feed the beast that is already gobbling up more than its share.

As well as or instead of these opportunities, there are other large book-selling platforms. IngramSpark is one. Draft2Digital is another. IngramSpark is a print and distribution company that supplies Print on Demand (POD) books either singly or in bulk, to bookshops and also—funnily enough—fulfils some orders for Amazon. IngramSpark also supplies digital copies of books to eReaders other than Kindle (Nook, Sony, Apple and Kobo). Draft2Digital now offers print services in partnership with IngramSpark but until recently it only offered digital book distribution. It can supply eBooks to Kindles, so if you prefer not to publish with KDP you can still reach readers who read on Kindles although your royalties will be reduced because both D2D *and* KDP will take a percentage.

I use both these platforms but I must say I have very limited sales. I do it more as an insurance policy than in the hope of selling vast numbers. It makes me feel that I have all the angles covered.

If you choose to enrol with Kindle Unlimited, you may not sell digital books on any other platform. Your eBook must be exclusively sold via KU on KDP.

This does not mean you cannot sell print books elsewhere. If you decide to go wide, IngramSpark is the best place to start.

As authors, we do have choices. We can try to sell our books by making personal approaches to independent booksellers in our area and offering our books on sale-or-return or heavily discounted. This is costly in terms of finances, involving buying and then storing our own print books in substantial quantities, and also in terms of time trudging from shop-to-shop trying to sell our wares. Being independently published will unfortunately always weigh against us, as book shop owners will assume we are no good because we have not been successful in getting an agent or a publisher. I have failed to get local bookshops to even assess my books, falling at the first 'Who's your publisher?' hurdle.

Alternatively, if you have a good website and a PayPal or similar account, you can sell directly. Again, you'd need to invest in stock and be able to store it, and be disciplined about processing orders and getting them sent out. Authors can buy their own books from Amazon and other platforms at a discounted price, usually cost plus postage, so there is profit to be made by selling direct. Theoretically it is possible to supply digital as well as print copies, by emailing an .ePub file. Again, some payment mechanism would be needed. This is something I intend to look into.

Many authors sell directly to the public at events and fairs, boot sales and craft shows. Once more, you need stock, a payment vehicle and confidence.

A. Publishing via IngramSpark (IS)

IS has a mixed reputation with indie authors. Some people seem to really like it, some find its platform difficult to navigate and its customer service very poor. Some hate it. I have seen multiple complaints about the print quality. Personally, I have found it ok to use. I have never ordered a print sample so I can't speak about the quality. I sell a mere handful of books, both print and eBook via IS, but at least when I go to local bookshops I can say that my books are available wholesale from IngramSpark.

Before starting this section, read through to make sure you have the answers to the various sections. Refer to the notes you wrote down for KDP and make sure you're being consistent.

i. Create an IS account and click on Add A Title.

ii. Choose print book only, eBook only or both. For this exercise, I'm going to choose both in order to talk you through it but it is debateable why you would need IS for eBooks if you are also going to use Draft2Digital.

iii. Click on I Have my Files Ready. Note the formats that IS requires.
- A print ready PDF of your print book jacket. Unfortunately IS requires a slightly different format for the cover file. Your graphic designer will help you produce a file to IS's specifications.
- A PDF for the print interior
- A JPG for the eBook cover and
- An .ePub file of your eBook interior.

Luckily, because of the way we formatted our files for KDP, we have all of these in our Files for Publication folder! You are ready to go!

iv. On the next screen you are invited to provide the book's title and ISBNs. You may use the ISBNs you gave for publishing to KDP and IS will have to transfer the details from KDP to ensure there is no duplication. IS will flag up if the ISBNs you supply have been used before (i.e. on KDP). You can have your ISBNs transferred but ONLY if you bought them yourself, NOT if you used the free one offered by KDP. Some authors upload and register their ISBN to IS first to avoid any delay involved in transferring, and publish on both platforms simultaneously. Note that IS does require an ISBN for eBooks whereas KDP does not.

v. It is always worth expanding the Show More Fields pane to add more information, such as a biography, other works and affiliations. If your book is a non-fiction book, for instance, and you are an expert in the field, book shops are going to be keener on stocking it if they see your qualifications and membership in professional associations.

vi. Subjects here is the same as Categories on KDP. Again, pick the best fit.

vii. Enter your blurb under Book Description and then Show More Fields to enter a shortened version which will be used in IS's book catalogues. Hopefully you created this when you wrote your blurb back in Chapter 8 point G.

viii. Within Show More Fields – Review Quotes, you can add excerpts from reviews that may now be trickling in from your launch team. Reviews from professional reviewers, like bloggers, count as **Editorial Reviews**, which arguably carry more weight. You can go back and add these as your blog tour progresses. Interestingly, these do find their way to the KDP listing, adding to its attraction to readers. You can add Editorial Reviews directly via KDP.

ix. Thema subjects help bookshops and libraries know how to categorise the book, for example, where to place it on a nonfiction shelf or how to group it within a genre.

x. Set your prices in accordance with the price you decided on for your KDP sales. Note that IS more or less insists that you offer a discount to wholesalers of up to 55%. Make sure that the discounted price does not result in a negative royalty for you. I always check the box for no returns.

xi. You will be invited to upload your files for print cover and print interior, eBook cover and eBook interior all at once. Here is where the Times New Roman (TNR) issue raises its head. IS will reject the print interior PDF if it has unembedded TNR in it. Hence, back in Chapter 9 Section A Point xi and in Section B, Point xxxvi I made such a big deal of it. The print-ready PDF for the cover may need tweaking by your graphic designer, but the .jpg for the eBook cover should be fine, as should your Kindle Create or Calibre generated .ePub. Once the files are uploaded, hit Continue and hold your breath. The next screen will show you if your files have been accepted.

xii. If they have, hurrah!

xiii. Check the requisite boxes to submit your book. That's it! Well done. You took the biggest step in going wide! In a few days you'll receive an email asking you to approve the IS proof. You can order a physical proof or view it on your screen. Either way, you must formally approve before your book will be enabled for distribution.

B. Publishing via Draft2Digital (D2D)

I do like D2D because it shows clearly the various eReader outlets, subscription services and library options where a book can be made available. It is easier to navigate than IS too. I haven't used them (so far) for print books. Once again, my sales on this platform are few because, frankly, Kindle has cornered the market on eReaders. However, why leave a sales stone unturned just because it is a small one?

i. Create a D2D account and select Start eBook. As I haven't used the print option, I will leave that for you to explore and concentrate on eBook creation here. D2D's print books are handled by IS in any case, so it could be argued that using D2D's print option is like throwing two stones at the same bird. It's worth reiterating that if you enrolled with KU on KDP you are not allowed to publish an eBook on any other platform, including this one.

ii. Work your way through the screens, entering all the information you are so familiar with by now. BISAC is a library and book shop cataloguing aid.

iii. On the next screen you can upload the .ePub and add a long and short description. Don't make these up on the hoof. Use the expanded and contracted versions of the blurb you wrote earlier. Use your own ISBN.

iv. The format required here is our old friend the .ePub, and because yours is a nice shiny new .ePub supplied by Kindle Create or Calibre, you won't need to faff around with D2D's formatting panes. Your title, chapter headings and so forth are already embedded within the .ePub. Upload the .ePub and the .jpg for the eBook cover. Don't be put off by D2D's suggestion that you'll miss out. You won't. If it's good enough for IS, it's good enough for D2D.

v. Select the sales channels. Look at all those subscription services and libraries you've never heard of! Remember NOT to select KDP if your book is already uploaded there, but note that if you ever didn't wish to publish directly with KDP, here is a way you could list your book for sale on Amazon having circumnavigated KDP. However, be aware that if you choose this option *both* D2D *and* Amazon will take cuts of your royalties. Of course, this is the case for all the sales outlets serviced by D2D.

It is entirely possible to upload your eBook *directly* to the other platforms such as Kobo, Sony, Barnes & Noble, Smashwords and Apple. I haven't done so, put off by the time it would take and also, frankly, due to formatting-fatigue by the time I've published with KDP and IS. There's no doubt there are advantages to going direct. Royalties will be more. You can participate in any promotions they offer, advertise directly to users of those platforms and enrol to their equivalent of KU. This might be one strong argument to outsourcing your formatting to a professional.

Having gone wide with both IS and D2D you've given your book its best chance of exposure in all marketplaces. In my experience, KDP will always be the best, but having other bases covered can't be a bad thing. What if Steven Spielberg reads on Nook? What if Jane Campion is a member of her local library? You've made it all the more possible for them, and people like them, to encounter your book.

11. Launch

To launch a book is not the same as to publish one. Publishing a book is releasing it onto a sales platform and thus the market for sale, which you can do with the same ease and about the same dramatic impact as squeezing toothpaste from a tube. For celebrity authors or those with established fan bases, mere publication will be enough to catapult a book into the stratosphere of the market, but for the rest of us who are less well known, and especially for debut writers, books need a launchpad and a rocket to propel them far enough into space that they stand a chance of getting into orbit.

The two essential ingredients are publicity and (good) reviews. Without these two things, your book will fail to leave the ground. I speak from experience. My first five books were published without publicity or reviews and were greeted with barely a whimper.

Publicity (advertising)

We are all used to having our social media feeds infiltrated by adverts and sponsored products these days and it is scary how they seem to know exactly what we are interested in. This is down to algorithms—the system that sellers use to decide how to show products in customers' search results. I don't know about you but I've been lured into clicking those links—swayed by the many positive endorsements—and gone on to buy the products. Then, having shown an interest, I'm inundated with more ads for similar things! This is annoying—but compelling—proof that the mysterious online algorithms work, and a reminder that we need to harness their power to sell our books.

Social media is a powerful tool for publicising what we have to sell. I am by no means an expert. It seems to me that in order to maintain a vibrant presence you have to be prepared to share everything about yourself, as well as your books. Frankly, I haven't the time or the inclination to post videos of my dogs playing on the beach, every cocktail I consume or the scenery around my house. I won't contribute to the fallacy that my life is perfect. Unfortunately, the act of writing isn't very interesting to watch. So I stick to images of my books with the occasional excerpt or review quote. That's my choice. I'm sure that, if I were to leverage it better, I'd have a larger following and reach more readers. Instagram, Twitter, TikTok and Facebook are powerful tools in the hands of the writer who is prepared to put in the time and effort. I'm just not that writer, but you might be.

Reviews

When did you last buy anything without reading a handful of reviews about it? Even if you didn't buy your washing machine or lawn mower online, I bet you googled some reviews of the various models before you went out shopping. Reviews are crucial to selling anything these days and that's why we need them.

My approach to gaining reviews is via a launch group. This gives the initial boost that fuels the launch. After that, I find the reviews trickle in from readers.

As a new author, you can source more reviews in a variety of ways. Goodreads has a Review Group which involves a group of ten writers reading and reviewing each other's books but crucially avoiding reciprocity. You read and review four books. Four other writers read and review yours. I used this group with some success in the beginning and made some lovely indie friends there.

NetGalley is a paid-for service that offers your book for free to reviewers, bloggers, librarians and booksellers. They apply to receive a copy and you can decide if you think they will be a good fit for your book by checking their profile and previous reviews.

Readers' Favourite allows you to upload your book and offer it free to reviewers who are registered with them.

However you do it, work hard on accumulating reviews for your book because they really matter.

These two modern-day phenomena—promotion/adverts and reviews—when applied properly, are absolutely key and, when worked in tandem, produce results. Promoting a book will always garner more interest and sales than not promoting it. Having a good number of positive reviews is better encouragement to the prospective buyer than having few or no reviews. Your blog tour and your promotions/adverts will bring prospective buyers to your book, but if it has no or few reviews, or if those reviews are lacklustre, the buyers may well pass it by. But if people are interested enough to check the book out and then see that it already has several glowing endorsements, they are much more likely to risk buying it.

What's more, success breeds success. Part of the Amazon algorithm is a calculation which divides the number of visitors to a book's page by the number of people who click on it to buy. A high conversion rate of visits to clicks will get their immediate interest. If something is selling well—making them money—they will promote it still further to people who have searched for or bought similar items, or bought from that seller (author) before. A tipping point is reached after which Amazon will begin to promote your book *for* you. They send out emails, bringing your book to the attention of targeted customers. 'We noticed you bought/searched for Alice Munro's books, so we thought you'd like these by Allie Cresswell because they're similar.' 'You've bought Allie Cresswell's books in the past. We thought you'd like to know she's written a new one.'

In the trade there is something called the also-bought or the also-read. You'll see, beneath the product you're considering, a whole marquee of items that others considered or bought alongside that one. They are comparing your buying and browsing habits with other people's. Jane and Louise both buy the same kind of moisturiser from Amazon. Jane also buys your book. Suddenly, Louise finds that your book is being recommended to her.

This is when your whole package comes together.

- Your book's title, cover and description immediately engage interest and inspire trust
- The (positive) reviews encourage them to buy

The more you sell, the more Amazon itself will promote your book and, unlike your paid-for promotions, this will be free.

There are sites where reviews are offered for a fee. Not only does this contravene Amazon's policy but the review will be specious—not a genuine response to the book. Some author groups offer review exchanges. This can be OK so long as there is no reciprocity—that is, you do not review a book by a writer who has reviewed you. Amazon takes a dim view of reciprocal reviews. If you join one of these groups, be sure there will be no pressure for you to post a favourable review. Goodreads has an excellent review group which uses a formula to ensure that there are no tit-for-tat reviews and that all reviews are unbiassed. The best way to get reviews is as I have described it: via a gradual and organic growth in your fanbase and your connections with the tribe.

I have a four-pronged approach to launch.

A. The blog tour
B. The launch team
C. Paid-for promotions
D. Pricing Strategies

For A and B, your hard work making contacts amongst other writers, readers, reviewers and bloggers now comes into its own, so I hope that you began this right back at the beginning.

A. Blog Tour

A blog tour is a virtual book tour. Rather than you touring the country, visiting book shops and literary festivals to do book signings, a group of book bloggers tell their hundreds or even thousands of followers about your book online. Hopefully you followed some book bloggers on Twitter and Instagram, liked and shared their posts and made meaningful comments so that by the time you make an approach asking them to feature your book, they have a sense of connection with you.

Some book bloggers make podcasts. I haven't explored this yet but I think it's going to be big.

Book bloggers are busy, busy people and often have their schedules mapped out weeks or even months in advance. Once you know your approximate launch date (see Chapter 12), begin to reach out and make contact. Send the book blurb and the cover to entice the blogger. Mention one of their posts you especially liked.

Alternatively, approach a blog tour organiser. Search on Twitter for Rachel's Random Resources @rareresourses or Kelly Lacey @KellyALacey. Tell them I sent you. Many more blog tour organisers exist. They will organise your tour for you, for a fee. Again, begin to set this up as soon as you know your launch date, and be prepared to be flexible as, again, they are busy and may not be able to fit you in exactly when you want. In fact, it might pay to book your blog tour first and determine your launch date in the light of it.

Ideally, your tour will take place over a few days, beginning a day or so after your launch, so that by the time the bloggers post, your book already boasts the reviews of your launch team. The blog's followers are more likely to buy the book if the blogger gave it a glowing endorsement AND it has a plethora of 5* reviews AND it is being sold at a discounted price.

The tours I have been on featured up to three bloggers per day over a period of four days to a week depending on how many bloggers I could get on board. Some bloggers will ask for the .ePub ARC so that they can read and review your book. This can be terrifying because these people don't owe you anything. They are avid readers and they know a good book from a poor one. You'll feel like you're throwing your child into a lion's den but think back to the dozens of classic books you've devoured in order to hone your writing skills. Recall the great indie writers you've tried to emulate. Remember the months or even years that your book has been in development, the hours of care you've poured into it, the opinions and input of alpha and beta readers and your editor. By now, but for the odd typo, the book is the very best iteration of itself and it's ready for a wider audience. Believe in it. Believe in yourself. It's time to see if this bird has wings.

Some bloggers will ask for an excerpt with a brief introduction, or provide a list of questions for you to answer. Others may ask you to write an article that will be unique to their blog. They will let you know how many words it should be. Think over aspects of the book and then write a few paragraphs on each aspect. For instance, what inspired you? What is your connection with the book's setting? Why did you want to explore those themes? Remember this is your opportunity to get people interested in your book. Let your enthusiasm shine through.

Regardless of what content they request, all the bloggers will require the following:

- Your book's title, blurb and a cover image.
- Its purchase links. These will be available to you pre-publication if you offered your book for pre-order but otherwise not until it is published. This is one of the reasons I recommend you publish your print book very quietly a couple of weeks before you publish the e version of it, so that you can get those purchase links. Check which country the blogger is in, and send the appropriate link for their country. Google Amazon.au, Amazon.ca, Amazon.in, Amazon.uk etc and then search for your book. Copy and paste the address in the Google search bar. People are lazy. They might find the idea of the book very interesting but unless you give them a link there and then to search for it and buy it, they might well forget. Always ensure the bloggers have links to add to their posts.
- A brief bio of you, the writer, and a picture.
- The .ePub file or the other content (excerpt etc) they have requested. Some bloggers only read print books

and will provide you with their address. For these, order an author copy of your book and send it directly to them. This is a cost to you, so you may wish to limit the number of print ARCs you supply.

Be business-like and professional in all your dealings with bloggers. They are super-busy people who often blog as a hobby alongside many other personal and professional commitments. They don't appreciate being messed around and are unlikely to host you again in future if you let them down.

Make a spreadsheet showing the bloggers you approached, who said yes and who said no. List their blog address and, if they provide it, their email address. Make a note that confirms what you sent and when you sent it.

No reputable blogger will ask for payment for a blog post. A blog tour organiser will charge a fee.

You can rely on the bloggers to do the rest. Having said that I usually check in with them a week or so before the scheduled date to make sure they have everything in place. Check their blog pages on their appointed day and make a note-to-self if you're happy with the way they featured your book. Unfortunately, some use spoilers, others write literary critiques rather than reviews. Save this information for next time. Always thank them personally for their contribution. Some bloggers allow their followers to make comments. Make sure you check in to interact with readers if possible. You might wish to ask some bloggers if you can use excerpts from their reviews for promotional purposes.

B. Launch Team
This is a group of readers who will commit to reading an ARC (Advance Review Copy) of the book, which they will receive free. In return, they agree to post an honest review on Amazon (crucially) plus **Goodreads**, **BookBub** and any other sites you stipulate for them ON LAUNCH DAY. The timing is critical. I can't emphasise this too much. A big splash of reviews piling

in on launch day will kickstart the Amazon algorithm, meaning that Amazon then begins to tell readers about your book.

A good launch team size is about twenty, but the more the merrier. Fewer than twenty leaves you vulnerable because, unfortunately, some will inevitably let you down and some reviews may be disallowed by Amazon. Bear in mind that some team members may post their reviews on national platforms of Amazon other than your own, so twenty team members may not mean twenty reviews on the same Amazon platform.

Make sure that your team members really *are* readers, not just nosey neighbours and acquaintances who are too polite to refuse. Ask them to point you to some of their previous reviews.

Not everyone can review on Amazon; there is a minimum spend before this is allowed, $50 in the US, £40 in the UK as of writing. As enthusiastic as they may be to get involved, there really is no point in giving away free copies of your book to people who cannot reciprocate with that all-important review.

Also, don't rely too heavily on your friends and family. Amazon knows when we are personally connected with someone (it's easy for them to check Facebook, for instance). They are unlikely to allow a review from someone who lives at the same address as you or who has the same name because, not unreasonably, they will assume the review is biased. Because I have had Amazon deliver gifts to my grandchildren at my son's address, my daughter-in-law is banned from reviewing my books.

Ideally, the launch team should be the equivalent of the brand reps who support small businesses on Instagram. Team members get free or discounted stuff in return for being a vocal advocate of that brand. Dipping into your new network of indie writer friends is a good idea. Offering to do a reciprocal beta read at some point is a helpful incentive but BEWARE as Amazon is alert to writers who review each other, and often removes reviews they think are not genuine.

Setting up a private Messenger chat group, WhatsApp group or Facebook page for your team is a good idea. Other writers can mingle with real readers. Readers get all starry-eyed over meeting real writers. Everyone is on board and excited about your project.

Involve your team in elements of the book's development by bouncing cover and blurb ideas off them and sharing snippets of the story. Keep in touch with them individually via Messenger or other messaging apps. You need this team. They get a free book but in reality they probably don't need that as much as you need their prompt and hopefully glowing review. Make sure they know how much you appreciate them.

Make a spreadsheet of their names and email addresses.

About five weeks before the launch, distribute an .ePub of the book to each launch team member. You may have used Kindle Create to format your book for Kindle, or Calibre. Either way, you will have an .ePub version of your book to distribute to the team.

The team will need to get that file to their e-reader, as follows:

Each individual who owns a Kindle has a unique Kindle email address. It will likely be theirname@kindle.com. This can be found by going to their Kindle's settings and then clicking Personalise. *You*—the author—cannot send the file directly to their Kindle email address as only the address they used to set up their Kindle (and probably their Amazon account) is permitted to do that. *They* must forward the .ePub file you send them to their Kindle email. It is quite likely that Amazon will send them an email asking if they're sure they want to add the book to their Kindle library. Saying Yes will cause the book to arrive and they can read it like any other Kindle book.

Team members who don't read on Kindle may request a PDF copy they can read on their tablet or PC. The PDF you created for print will be great for this. Again, attach it to an email. Or, if you decided not to produce a print version, you can simply

Save As your eBook Master in PDF format. Those who use other kinds of e-reader (Nook, Kobo) should be able to send the .ePub file to their device.

I usually send the file attached to an email with a polite but pointed reminder that they are receiving a *free* copy of the book *in return* for their honest review, posted on *Amazon* plus any other platforms *on the launch date we have agreed*. I remind them that the book is copyrighted and should not be shared or forwarded to anyone else. Using the Receive flag on the email will confirm that the email (and the file) have both been received, but usually the recipients are courteous enough to let you know.

I make a note on my spreadsheet of the date the file was sent to each team member.

It's well worth asking the team to let you know if they find typos or other errors in the book. Be ready for some to read with a fine-toothed comb and others to find none at all. Others will mistakenly act as though they are beta readers, and give you a much more detailed critique than is really required at this stage. Each time you receive a note, go to your dated Master Print file and your dated Master eBook file. Use the Find function and make the corrections. Make sure these two Master files are always updated in sync. Don't re-upload to the sales platforms at this stage until you're sure that you've swept up all the mistakes that might still be hiding in the manuscript. Of course, you'll get notes from several people about the same errors, but thank each one.

A couple of weeks before launch, while your team is reading the ARC, forewarn them that the day after Publication Date (not launch date), you will reduce the book to 99p/c for one day only. If they choose to, they can buy the book at this discounted price. If they do a flick-through 'read' on their Kindle the page reads will count towards your KU payment—assuming the reader is enrolled in KU. If not, their review will show as Verified—meaning it's from a person who actually bought the book. I'm not 100% convinced that this makes much difference as both verified and non-verified reviews appear side by side, but better safe than sorry. The reviews of those who choose not to buy the book will still count and are still vital to your launch. A person does not need to have bought the book on Amazon to review it on Amazon providing they meet the minimum spend requirement.

See the list of timings in Chapter 12 for how and when to reduce your book's price for this and any other promotions you have signed up for.

Encourage your team to let each other know how they are getting on with the book via your social media page or launch team message group. Keep the hype up if you can, reminding them always of the date of the launch and how important their reviews are to the success of the book.

On launch day, ask the team to post their reviews to Amazon, Goodreads and any other sites they know of and then share a link to their review on the team page. Check these off against your spreadsheet so you know who has come through and who has let you down.

Be sure to thank each person individually for their contribution and ask them if you can call on them again in the future. Encourage them to share their review on their own social media feeds so that their friends and family and work colleagues know of their involvement and also of course about the book.

C. Promotions

Paid-for promotion is a way of publicising the book to a wide audience. Promoting a book that already has those all-important review ratings is more likely to generate sales than promoting one with no reviews or ratings.

Ideally, paid-for promotions should occur a few days or up to a week after launch day, so that the reviews can be in place.

Promo-stacking is better than having them all on one day. Stacking means having the promotions follow each other. It's a horizontal stack rather than a vertical one. It also helps you determine which promos have been most effective. Check your sales each day by visiting your KDP dashboard and choosing Reports to see how each promo impacts sales. Amazon only registers sales immediately for eBooks. For print books, the sale is posted on the day the book is shipped. This needs to be kept in mind when evaluating advertising, but realistically the majority of sales are likely to be eBooks.

David Gaughran, www.davidgaughran.com is a mine of useful information on promoting books, which he selflessly dispenses free of charge.

There are numerous book promotion sites that send information about your book to their subscribers. Book Cave, Fussy Librarian, Books Butterfly, ENT, ReaderIQ and Bargain Booksy are all sites I have used in the past, with some success. Some sites have thousands of subscribers. These promotions are reasonably priced and are well worth considering. Most of them will expect you to have reduced the price to 99p/c or even to nothing. Personally, I don't give my books away for free anymore, other than to the launch team. People love free things but they don't value them. They may well 'buy' a book that is free but not read it for weeks, months or ever. They rarely post a review. I haven't had many 1* reviews but I'm convinced the handful I've had have been from people who have taken advantage of a free promotion. They equate 'free' with 'valueless'. Often they admit to not having read the book beyond the first few pages! The only mitigation for giving a book away for nothing is that it will enhance your ranking within your category. If that matters to you, go for it.

Some promotion sites will promote books regardless of the quality of cover or spelling errors in the blurb. They don't discriminate and my feeling is that their members won't either. Join up and check out the site's promo posts. Do the books look good quality? Are there dozens in each category, or does it look as though someone has curated a select few? You can always unsubscribe if you don't like what you see.

Other sites will only promote books that have a certain number of 5* ratings. Accordingly—as it's impossible to accumulate these ratings until after your launch—it's hard to coordinate these promos to coincide with your launch, which ideally you want to do. You might consider delaying your promotion, or at least scheduling it on these sites a couple of weeks after your launch and blog tour are out of the way, but then you lose the impetus.

BookBub is the giant in the field. They are very selective about which books they will promote, but being picked by them is a sure-fire way of catapulting your book because BookBub members know that books promoted by them will be good. They are very picky and they charge a *lot* of money, so be prepared. I've never been successful in my applications but I keep on trying. BookBub also offers adverts, which are similar to Amazon adverts in that you bid and pay per click. This frightens me as it could run away while you're not looking.

Amazon and Facebook adverts are also worth considering. Facebook in particular allows you to be specific about the audience for your advert, selecting people who are interested in your genre of book or who like authors of books similar to yours. You can differentiate by gender, age, geography and interest. You can set the budget, and it doesn't need to be large.

I've had less success with Amazon ads. There seem to be so many variables and it's easy to spend lots of money without knowing it.

Thankfully, Written Word Media offers an Amazon ads package. I have used this and been pleased with the results.

There are lots and lots of companies who will offer to promote your book on Twitter and Instagram. They post several times a day for an agreed length of time. Some of them make ludicrous claims for your book. One of them described my gentle, Austen-inspired *Emma* prequel as 'a high velocity page-turner of a thriller that will have you afraid to switch the lights out at night' or some similar garbage. These packages are cheap but not very effective, in my experience.

Book promotion works with a shot-gun effect, scattering many thousands of emails, posts and tweets—some hit the spot although many go astray. It's a numbers game. There are many competing companies all trying to get you to pay them to promote your book. Finding the one that works for *you* is a different question.

Try a couple and see how they impact sales.

D. Pricing Strategies

I have mentioned several times that I do not give books away for nothing, but there is no doubt that discounting for a limited time is effective. Who doesn't love a bargain? A judicious reduction in the price of a book, especially if it coincides with the blog tour or a schedule of promotions, is a good strategy, providing yet one more inducement (along with the good reviews) for a reader to buy. Much depends on what price you initially decided on. If you went for what I would consider a high price for an eBook, say $9.99, a sudden reduction to $5.99 is going to look pretty attractive; but then, post-promotion, you're going to have to return the book to its original price. Personally, as my books are all over 100,000 words, I think $6.99 is a reasonable price to pay. I'd pay that amount for a book by an author I have read before or that has been recommended to me either by its reviewers or by a blogger whose opinion I trust. That's the price I invariably set at the start, and then for my launch I discount to $4.99 or even as low as $1.99 for a very short period, for a specific promotion, for instance. Where a new book is in a trilogy, I might discount the first book to £1.99, the second to $2.99 and the final (new) book to $4.99. That makes three books for just under $10.

I might discount from time to time to boost sales, when doing a Facebook advert or a flurry of Instagram posts. I usually pick books that aren't doing so well, but discounting slightly a book that is already flying off the shelves can also be a good idea. As I have a catalogue of books, getting a new reader is the biggest hurdle for me to overcome. If the reader enjoys that book, they are likely to return to buy others. Amazon will recommend more of my books to them and also to others who have a similar purchase history. There is nothing more encouraging to me than the phrase, 'My first Allie Cresswell book, but not my last,' in a new review.

Here is a screenshot of my Amazon sales for the 90-day period that included the launch of *The Widow's Weeds*. Note the spike of pre-orders on Publication Day and then the higher spike a few days later, a combination of the blog tour and my paid-for promotions.

You will see that sales returned to better than their previous levels after the launch.

Summary

In the end, the best way to sell books is to write very good ones and to get people to tell others how good they are. This may be via reviews, word of mouth, blogs or paid-for promotion.

Another method to explore is **partners**. Here, you leverage your own mailing list or contacts by asking some of them to promote your book. Other writers with whom you feel you share genre, standards or audience may agree to promote your books to *their* fans and followers in return for you promoting theirs. A page on your website where you feature comparable books and writers, a weekly guest post on your social media stories, or a page at the back of your book where you mention the books of other writers can all be arranged reciprocally.

Periodically you might like to use one of the paid-for promotion companies to boost sales and exposure, reducing the book's price for the duration of the promotion. Coincide this promotion with a splurge on your social media feeds to revitalise interest in the book.

Any way you can get the word out there is good.

I met a writer this week who was standing in the car park at Haworth—birthplace of the Brontë sisters—selling his own books in return for free, all-day parking. He told me that by this means alone he had sold 30,000 copies of his books, which clearly he'd had printed himself. All profits were donated to charity. This kind of dedication and ingenuity has to be admired. If you can, consider taking a stall on a local market or craft fair and see how you get on. Of course, you'll have to invest in a goodly quantity of your own books, but if you don't believe in your books how can you expect others to? Self-promotion is the best kind of all.

12. Putting it All Together

Setting a timescale for the writing of a book is ridiculous. Writing a book takes as long as it takes. Some writers reckon to finish a book in a few weeks but I can't imagine they are very good. Others take years. Take your own time and write your own book, consulting a developmental editor once you've completed your first or second draft to help you get your story or project into shape. Use this creative period productively by networking amongst other indie writers and bloggers, joining book groups and getting to know the staff at your local bookshop. Set up an author Facebook page and begin to establish yourself as a keen reader by posting reviews and sharing about writers you admire.

Commissioning a copy or line editor is the first concrete step towards actual publication. If you've got that far then your project definitely has legs and you can really begin to plan its completion and launch. However, it might be problematic to set a publication and launch date until the editor agrees to a date by which they will return the edited manuscript. Your own individual commitments will determine how long it takes to make the corrections and alterations decreed by the edit.

Sallianne Hines' book, *About Editing. An essential guide for authors*, the companion to this book, gives very helpful estimates of the time required for each kind of edit you might commission.

The other variable is the availability of bloggers for the tour. I usually contact my bloggers a good three months in advance of the date I hope to launch, to invite them to take part and to pencil in a date for their blog post. Even then, sometimes they are booked up already.

Taking this into consideration, generally I can take the date the editor commits to completing the copy edit as a baseline to plan the launch. I allow about six weeks from the return of the manuscript to me from the editor. My editor is extremely accommodating about sending the edited manuscript back in tranches so that I can work on it in parallel, but not all editors will agree to this.

So, whatever date my editor promises to have the finished manuscript back to me, I can pencil in my publication six weeks after that and my launch about four days later. The blog tour and paid-for promos will begin around five days after that, depending on the bloggers' availability and what dates I can book the promos.

I use the calendar on my PC to pencil in the dates.

With a date in mind I can begin to firm up the launch team by letting them know what schedule I'm looking at. Can they commit to read and review by that date? They might be on holiday, or heavily involved at work, or undergoing hospital treatment. Any of these might preclude them. If that's the case they need to be weeded out, thanked, and promised a place on the team for the next book. And they need to be replaced. They themselves might recommend their replacement.

So, the timeline, from the day I feel my book is as finished as I on my own can make it (see Chapter 8 Section A), looks like this:

<u>Week 1</u> – Read aloud to the alpha reader and make amendments accordingly. See Chapter 8.

<u>Weeks 2 & 3</u> – Beta and sensitivity readers get to work. Meanwhile, I research covers and cover designers, brief the chosen cover artist and interview editors, then commission an editor. See Chapters 8 & 11.

<u>Week 4</u> – Input beta-suggested alterations and redraft as required, then send to the editor. See Chapters 8 & 11.

<u>Weeks 5, 6, 7 & 8</u> (or longer, as agreed) – While the editor is at work, I finalise the cover design and possibly begin the KDP print book-creation process using a Placeholder document, and write the blurb. See Chapters 8, 9 & 11.

Weeks 9 & 10 – Once I receive the edited manuscript my six-week countdown begins. I input the edits, being careful not to make new errors by not deleting properly, leaving repeated words or messing up the case or tense of verbs. Then I upload the edited manuscript to Kindle Create or Calibre in order to produce .ePub. I send the .ePub to the launch team and the bloggers who have agreed to review. See Chapter 9.

Weeks 11, 12, 13 & 14 – While the ARCs are with the launch team and the bloggers, I format, proofread and upload the book as Placeholder to KDP, saving as Draft or, for the eBook, choosing the Pre-order option. Be prepared to do this several times as the team will inevitably come back with typos etc and as you get the margins right for the print version. If Pre-order has been chosen, this provides the all-important purchase link (the link to your pre-order) that can be sent to bloggers as well as other content as listed in Chapter 11 Section A. If pre-order has not been chosen, during Week 13, when the manuscript is as perfect as possible, publish the print book. Then send the print book purchase link and all other information to bloggers. See Chapters 9 & 11.

Five days before Publication Day is the cut-off point for any alterations to the eBook pre-order (if you've chosen that). The final .ePub file must be uploaded by then.

Week 15 – **Publication Day.** Also called a Soft Launch Day. No bells, no whistles, no flags. This is either the day the eBook is manually published or the day determined by the pre-order. Nothing about the book's content or details can be altered in the five-day window before a pre-order goes live, including its price. Any who pre-ordered the book will pay full price for it. See Chapter 12.

Publication Day + 1. The day after publication (if the pre-order option has been used), or on Publication Day itself, return to the KDP dashboard and reduce the price of the eBook to 99p/c. You will be prompted to reduce the royalty share to 35% from 70%. KDP say it can take up to 72 hours for the price change to take effect, but I have never known it take more than 24.

The team should be reminded that the book is reduced and politely asked to buy it at this tiny price and to flick through the book, registering the page reads. If they are members of KU, their page-reads will count towards royalties. If not, their review will be Verified, meaning they actually bought the book. Some writers believe that Verified reviews count for more. Importantly, the ratio of visits to the page and clicks to buy will be almost 100%, just what Amazon's algorithm is looking for to kickstart its promotional efforts on your behalf.

Publication Day + 2. Return the eBook to its full price, or a discounted price if you have committed to this for the promotions, which you likely have. I never reduce my books to less than £1.99/$1.99 these days other than for the team. Leave it at this price for the duration of the blog tour and/or as long as your promotions and adverts run. For me, this would be about ten days.

Publication Day + 3. This is the final day for the team to flick through the book and finalise their reviews.

Publication Day + 4 is **Launch Day**. That is, the day the book is 'officially' launched out onto the world with *all* the bells, whistles and flags you can muster. This is the day when those reviews need to be posted, with busy traffic to the book's sales page on Amazon. It calculates the number of visits that result in a purchase, notices the instant popularity of the book and its profit-potential antenna begins to twitch. It sees that John, Sunita, Beryl and Mohammed and two dozen others have bought, read and are reviewing the book and it looks at the trends of their other purchases. Let's say John and Sunita are both big fans of Sarah Maine—and why wouldn't they be? Amazon makes a connection between readers who like Sarah Maine and readers who like my books and begins to recommend my books to those who buy Sarah Maine's. In addition, imagine this is the first book of mine that Beryl and Mohammed have read. Amazon will note they bought and liked this one and begin to recommend others to them from my back catalogue.

Allow a couple of days for the reviews to appear. Give a gentle reminder to those on the team who have not got round to it yet. I cannot emphasise sufficiently how crucial their participation is in this process. Any traffic the blog tour or the paid-for promos might send to the book's sale page will be wasted if it does not have a goodly quantity of positive reviews against it.

A few days after Launch Day, the blog tour kicks off and the promos begin. I book one promo a day for about a week or ten days.

Blog readers are guided to my book by the bloggers. Encouraged (hopefully) by the bloggers' enthusiasm, and attracted by the discounted price, they buy the book. The John-and-Sunita effect comes into play once more.

Paid-for promos that you might have booked with, say, Bargain Booksy or Book Cave, go live. Emails from those companies fall into the inboxes of those who have subscribed to them. They like the look of my book and click the link that takes them to its page on Amazon. The Beryl-and-Mohammed mountain begins to move.

And so it mushrooms over the course of the blog tour and the paid-for promos, with Amazon helpfully sending out emails to their customers to tell them about the book. As they buy, my book moves up the rankings within its category. That rings another bell in the Amazon firmament. 'This book's doing rather well, making us money. Let's give it a boost.' Happy days!

If this is your first book, let me say congratulations, and welcome to the indie tribe. You're one of us, now.

The next pages show a timetable of activities, a summary of all we have discussed, in an attempt to show how many tasks need to be tackled simultaneously.

As long as it takes	Write the book, 1st and 2nd draft.	Meanwhile, cultivate friends amongst the indie community by joining groups. Follow and interact with book bloggers. Join book groups and get to know the staff at your local bookshop. Set up an author Facebook page & other social media accounts.	See Chapters 3 & 4
	Developmental edit if required. Write third draft.	Meanwhile, begin to identify possible launch team members and 2 beta readers. Source sensitivity reader if needed.	See Chapters 5 & 11
Allow one week	Alpha read. Fourth draft.	Meanwhile, firm up launch team members.	See Chapter 8

Allow two weeks	Beta and sensitivity reads.	Meanwhile, research covers, brief cover artist and interview editors. Commission an editor. Based on editor's timescale, approach bloggers.	See Chapters 8 & 11
Allow one week	Input beta-suggested alterations and redraft as required. Send to editor.	Meanwhile finalise blog tour members & dates, thus setting publication & launch dates.	See Chapters 8 & 11
Allow four weeks or as agreed	Editor at work.	Meanwhile, finalise cover design, possibly begin the KDP print book creation process using Placeholder document. Write the blurb. Consult launch team re cover and blurb.	Chapters 8, 9 & 11
Allow two weeks	Input the edits.	When done, upload the edited manuscript to Kindle Create	Chapter 9

		or Calibre in order to produce .ePub ARC.	
Allow four weeks	Send ARCs to launch team & bloggers who are to review.	Meanwhile, format print & eBook and upload to KDP, saving as Draft or choose Pre-order. Repeat as further notes from team come in.	Chapters 9 & 11
During fourth week (above)	Publish print book ensuring all errors are corrected. Send print book purchase link and all other information to bloggers.	Meanwhile, remind team that book will be reduced and encourage them to buy and flick through.	Chapters 9 & 11
Publication Day	Publish eBook or the day pre-order goes live.	Share the joy with team.	Chapter 12
Next day	Reduce price to 99p/c. It can take several hours for the price change to take effect.	Send link to team.	Chapter 12
Next day	Book is reduced. Team buys and flicks through.		Chapter 12
Next day	Return price to normal or		Chapter 12

	discounted for promos.		
Launch Day	Team posts reviews.	Encourage and thank team members.	Chapter 12
Next 2-3 days	Reviews begin to appear	Share reviews on social media.	Chapter 12
Next day and for duration of tour and promos	Blog tour and paid-for promos commence.	Share reviews on social media, tweet and post on Instagram. Encourage family and friends to share. Update team re rankings and successes.	Chapters 11 & 12
Following days	Upload book to other platforms.		Chapter 10

13. Jargon Busting Glossary of Terms.

.ePub. A computer file compatible with eReaders (Electronic Reading Devices)

Algorithm. The systems that Amazon and other online sellers use to decide how to show products in search results, influenced by what *else* that person has already bought, and what *others*, who bought this, also searched for.

Alpha Read. The book's first non-professional reader, who identifies broad areas for improvement, erroneous details, plot holes and pacing issues.

ARC. Advance Review Copy. A copy of the book sent out before publication to the launch team, reviewers or bloggers. It is tacitly understood that the ARC may still contain some editorial issues.

Beta Read. The book's second reader(s) who look for more nuanced issues including character development and arc, plot motivations and inconsistencies, assuming the major issues raised by the alpha-reader have been dealt with.

Bio. A biography that describes your journey to being a writer.

Blog Tour. A virtual/online book tour where the book is featured on several book blogs, usually three per day for about five days or a week.

Blurb. The description that appears on the back of the print book and on its sales page on online bookstores.

BookBub. A forum for readers that monetises by offering advertising and promotion deals to authors.

D2D. An abbreviation of Draft2Digital, a book selling platform.

Calibre. A programme that will format a manuscript into an .ePub so as to provide the functionality of the Kindle eReader.

eBook. The digital version of a book.

Editorial Review. A review from a professional such as a newspaper arts and culture correspondent or a blogger. Note that these should never ask for payment.

Embedded. Fonts that are embedded cannot be altered or substituted in later versions of the document. If you have used unusual fonts, these may get altered to default fonts if not embedded.

Going Wide. Industry slang for selling on platforms other than KDP.

Goodreads. An online forum for readers where they can get recommendations, post reviews and discuss books. It is owned by Amazon.

Gutter. The inner margin of a print book, where the pages meet the spine, ensuring that print does not disappear into the thickness of the book binding.

Hybrid publisher. A publishing house that will charge you a percentage of the costs to produce your book and take a proportion of your royalties.

Indie. Independently published.

IS. Abbreviation for IngramSpark, who are the dominant worldwide wholesale book distributor from which bookstores and libraries order.

ISBN. International Standard Book Number. Every version of every book must have a unique ISBN.

JPEG. Joint Photographic Experts Group. An image compression method that is the most popular for online images.

KDP. Kindle Direct Publishing is Amazon's platform for self-publishing books—eBooks, paperbacks, hardbacks and large print—for sale on Amazon's global network of online stores.

Kindle Create. A programme provided by KDP that will format a manuscript into a .KPF and an .ePub so as to provide the functionality of the Kindle eReader.

Kindle. The electronic reading device (eReader) that is compatible with digital books downloaded from Amazon. Other eReaders are available, such as Kobo, for books downloaded from the Rakuten Kobo online bookstore, and Nook for books bought from the Barnes & Noble online platform.

.KPF. A Kindle Package File created by the Kindle Create programme and KDP's preferred format for eBook uploads.

KU. Kindle Unlimited. A subscription service on Amazon that allows people to download a certain number of books per month for free, on payment of a monthly subscription. The author gets paid per page read.

Launch. The day the book's marketing begins.

Literary agent. A person who will represent you, presenting your book to publishers and assist you with contract negotiations. They generally take between 10 - 15% of your royalties.

Metadata. Details about your book such as its title and subtitle, categories and keywords that help KDP catalogue it correctly for sale.

Partners. Other writers, editors, bloggers or industry influencers who agree to feature your book on their website or social media stories. You could return the favour.

PDF. Portable Document Format, for files that are fixed and cannot be altered but can be easily shared.

POD. Print on demand. Books are printed off to order, one at a time, as opposed to hundreds or thousands to be kept in warehouses.

Pre-order. A service offered by KDP whereby customers can order the eBook version of your novel ahead of publication.

They pay full price and the book drops into their Kindle library on the day of publication. Importantly, your book gets a sales page on Amazon which provides you with a link, essential for planning blog tours and promotions.

Purchase link. A link to your book's sales page on Amazon, where customers can buy it. Essential to provide a purchase link to book bloggers and promotion companies so they can send traffic to the book's page.

Publication. The day the book goes live on a book site. Also known as a Soft Launch.

Self-publishing. The author publishes his or her own work at their own cost, taking responsibility for the content, quality and marketing and reaping 100% of any rewards.

Sensitivity reader. An expert or someone with personal or professional knowledge of things outside the writer's experience—such as race, sexuality, disability—where the misrepresentation of such things might cause offense or be politically sensitive.

Synopsis. A complete summary of what happens in the book.

TNR. An abbreviation for Times New Roman font.

Traditional publisher. A publisher who will invest in your work and pay for its production, getting their remuneration from any book sales.

Triggers. Incidents or themes that might 'trigger' a reader's anxiety, addiction, flashbacks, PTSD or other conditions.

Vanity press. A publisher who produces a book but charges 100% of the costs of production to the author, bearing no costs and no risks themselves. They have no interest in the quality of the book or whether it sells any copies. Literally, these presses simply massage the ego of the writer.

Thank you

for buying this book. I hope it has helped you navigate your way through the writing, formatting, uploading and launching procedures.

As a self-published author I don't have the support of a marketing department behind me. I rely on you, the reader, to spread the word. Please return to the platform where you purchased this book and leave a short review. Reviews are essential to the writer—you know this by now—and provide a helpful indication to others who might be considering buying the book.

I'd like to thank my fellow-author, editor and friend Sallianne Hines for her encouragement and support as we put together our complementary books.

About the Author

Allie Cresswell was born in Stockport, UK and began writing fiction as soon as she could hold a pencil.

She did a BA in English Literature at Birmingham University and an MA at Queen Mary College, London.

She has been a print-buyer, a pub landlady, a book-keeper, run a B & B and a group of boutique holiday cottages. Nowadays Allie writes full time.

She has two grown-up children, two granddaughters, two grandsons and two cockapoos but just one husband—Tim. They live in Cumbria, NW England.

Allie has self-published fourteen novels and two anthologies.

About Self-publishing. An essential guide for new authors is her first non-fiction book.

Find her on Facebook. Visit www.allie-cresswell.com. Follow her on Twitter @alliescribber or on Instagram @allienovelist.

Also by Allie Cresswell

Game Show

Relative Strangers

Crossings

Tiger in a Cage

The Cottage on Winter Moss

The Hoarder's Widow

The Widow's Mite

The Widow's Weeds

The House in the Hollow

The Lady in the Veil

Tall Chimneys

Mrs Bates of Highbury

The Other Miss Bates

Dear Jane

www.ingramcontent.com/pod-product-compliance
Lightning Source LLC
Chambersburg PA
CBHW071409080526
44587CB00017B/3230